The Greatest Weddings
of All Time

People

Contents

76

Staff

Editor **ELIZABETH SPORKIN** Senior Editor **NANCY STEDMAN** Art Director **RINA MIGLIACCIO** Chief of Reporters **TOBY KAHN** Picture Editor **BRIAN BELOVITCH** Writers **VICTORIA BOUGHTON, DANIELLE DUBIN, ELIZABETH O'BRIEN, JOANNA POWELL, LISA RUSSELL, JENNIFER WULFF** Associate Art Director **RONNIE BRANDWEIN-KEATS** Reporters **RANDY VEST (Deputy), SARA DOWNEY, RENNIE DYBALL, EMILY HEBERT** Copy Editor **TOMMY DUNNE** Operations **HELEN RUSSELL** Special thanks to: Jane Bealer, Robert Britton, Lisa Burnett, Sal Covarrubias, Urbano DelValle, Sally Foster, Margery Frohlinger, Rebecca Gaffney, George Hill, Patricia Hustoo, Lance Kaplan, Salvador Lopez, Maddy Miller, Eric Mischel, Gregory Monfries, Charles Nelson, Lillian Nici, Susan Radlauer, Deborah Ratel, Mikema Reape, Patricia Rommeney, Annette Rusin, John A. Silva, Ann Tortorelli, Cynthia Vaccina, Céline Wojtala, Patrick Yang, Peter Zambouros

President **ROB GURSHA** Vice President, Branded Businesses **DAVID ARFINE** Executive Director, Marketing Services **CAROL PITTARD** Director, Retail & Special Sales **TOM MIFSUD** Director of Finance **TRICIA GRIFFIN** Marketing Director **KENNETH MACLLUM** Prepress Manager **EMILY RABIN** Associate Book Production Manager **SUZANNE DeBENEDETTO** Associate Product Manager **SARA STUMPF** Assistant Product Manager **LINDA FRISBIE** Special thanks to: Robert Dente, Gina Di Meglio, Anne-Michelle Gallero, Peter Harper, Natalie McCrea, Jessica McGrath, Jonathan Polsky, Mary Jane Rigoroso, Steven Sandonato, Bozena Szwagulinski, Niki Whelan

An Irish castle on a delicious June day. A fairy-tale gown

The Greatest

concocted from 40 yards of silk taffeta, crinoline and

Weddings

heirloom lace. A grand entrance with gold dust and rose

of

petals on the floor. Fireworks lighting up a Malibu cliff.

All Time

Here's to the glamor and grace of 92 celebrity weddings.

Grace Kelly & Prince Rainier III

AT 26, GRACE KELLY WAS AN OSCAR-winning movie star and a world-class beauty. Though she had dated the likes of Clark Gable and William Holden, it would take nothing less than a monarch to match her wattage in matrimony. Fortunately, one day her prince did come, in the person of Rainier III, titled ruler of the tiny, well-heeled principality of Monaco. Her first meeting with the prince—a 45-minute visit to his 13th-century pink palace arranged as a photo op by *Paris Match* while she was attending the Cannes Film Festival—left Kelly charmed. After an eight-month-long correspondence, he visited her family in Philadelphia on Christmas, and she agreed to become his princess. "He is everything I've ever loved," the actress said.

The Roman Catholic mass took place under a sunny Monaco sky the morning after a civil ceremony required by law. Some 600 guests, including Cary Grant, Ava Gardner and Aristotle Onassis, were riveted as the bride entered the Cathedral of St. Nicholas. She was breathtaking in a gown fashioned by movie costumer Helen Rose out of ivory silk taffeta, *peau de soie* and 125-year-old lace. While cameras from MGM studios rolled, she floated down the aisle. Prince Rainier, 32, followed her to the altar, as royal custom dictated. Later, guests repaired to the palace courtyard.

The mother of three headline-garnering children, Princess Grace became a major presence in Monaco, winning the devotion of her subjects. "She's still everywhere," her husband said years after her 1982 death.

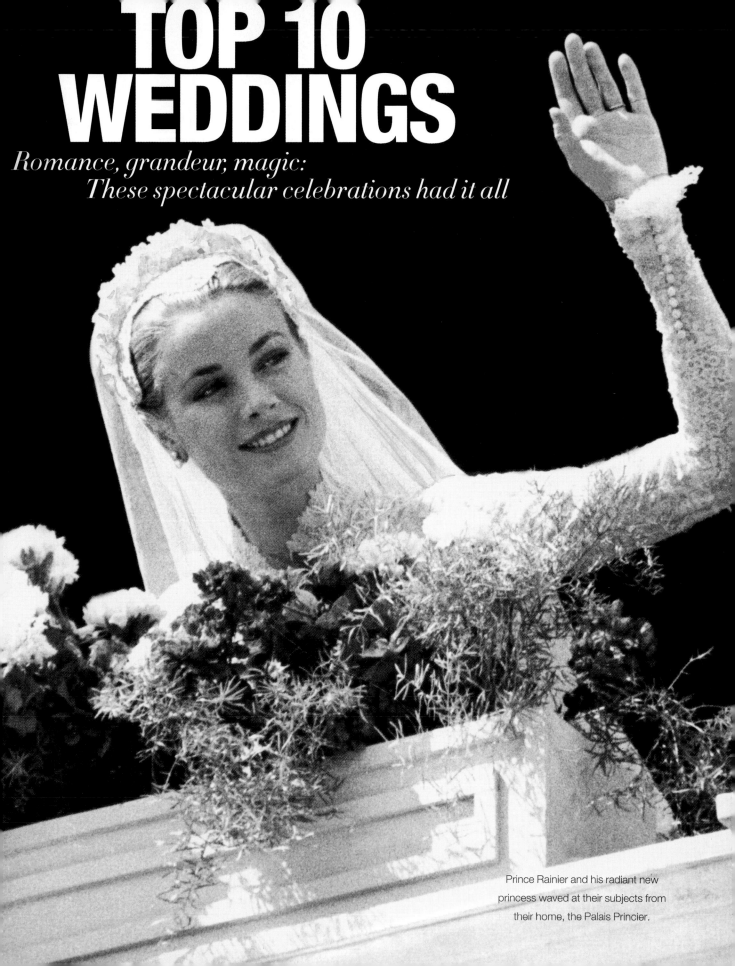

TOP 10 WEDDINGS

Romance, grandeur, magic:
These spectacular celebrations had it all

Prince Rainier and his radiant new
princess waved at their subjects from
their home, the Palais Princier.

The altar was festooned with white hydrangeas, lilacs and lilies.

The 5'6½" Kelly wore low pumps so that she wouldn't tower over the 5'7" prince.

For the luncheon, the bridal party and close family sat in a large room at the palace.

The six bridesmaids wore yellow organdy dresses and matching wide-brimmed hats.

In a Lanvin gown the eve of the wedding, the princess-to-be (with mom Margaret) displayed royal elegance.

Queen Elizabeth & Prince Philip

THE WEDDING OF SHY, PETITE PRINCESS Elizabeth to her handsome third cousin Philip gave a war-weary Britain something to get excited about. "People are tired of sadness, they need a party; they are tired of hate, they need to think of love," said novelist Rebecca West. Many British citizens, still suffering from war shortages, selflessly forwarded their clothing rations to help Elizabeth (who was also subject to rationing) obtain the most extravagant gown possible. On her wedding day, the 21-year-old princess entered Westminster Abbey to a fanfare of trumpets. Resplendent in a long-sleeved satin dress embroidered with thousands of pearls, she walked down the crimson-carpeted aisle to the altar, where she exchanged vows with the British-raised Philip, 26, a Danish aristo-crat whom she had loved since she was 13. Said her governess: "Things had at last gone right for her."

After the wedding, Elizabeth and Philip rode to Buckingham Palace for the traditional meal.

The ceremony was the first royal wedding broadcast on radio.

Hundreds of thousands took in the pageantry.

A Botticelli painting inspired the gown.

The Duke of Windsor & Wallis Simpson

FOR 11 MONTHS, KING EDWARD VIII RULED Britannia. Then the monarch abdicated his throne to marry the object of his infatuation—Wallis Simpson, a divorcée whom he, as head of the Church of England, was forbidden to wed. "Nobody has ever given up what he did for a woman," declared their friend C.Z. Guest. Ostracized by the British royals, 42-year-old Edward (demoted to Duke of Windsor) and his 40-year-old American bride sought refuge in France, where they exchanged vows in an Anglican ceremony at the Château de Candé in the Loire Valley. Wallis's widely copied silk crepe outfit by Mainbocher was the epitome of understated elegance. After the wedding luncheon, the couple began their travels together—first stop Austria—taking 300 pieces of luggage with them onto the Orient Express.

A newsreel cameraman captured the couple after the ceremony.

The dashing duke wore a white carnation; the stylish duchess pinned an Art Deco brooch to her collar.

Prince Charles & Diana Spencer

FOR MANY, THE UNION OF BRITAIN'S PRINCE Charles and Diana Spencer was the wedding of the century. And though history has dimmed its dazzling memory, it enthralled the world with its pomp and pageantry (and $52 million price tag). By horse-drawn glass carriage, the 20-year-old coltish aristocrat, nicknamed Shy Di, arrived at London's glorious St. Paul's Cathedral with a tiny blue bow and an 18-karat-gold horseshoe sewn into the waistband of her dress—40 billowing yards of silk taffeta, crinoline and heirloom lace. "We wanted to make her look like a fairy-tale princess," said the gown's codesigner David Emanuel.

At the end of the 652-foot red carpet, in full Royal Navy regalia, stood her prince, 32, the heir to the British throne, waiting with the Archbishop of Canterbury and 2,500 guests. The 70-minute Anglican ceremony included three different choirs and a rousing version of "God Save the Queen." Two million cheering celebrants lined the streets on the route back to Buckingham Palace, where a traditional afternoon wedding "breakfast" of lobster, chicken and plenty of bubbly was held for 120 honored guests.

When the pair became the first royal newlyweds to seal the marriage with a public kiss on the palace balcony, no one could foresee such a storybook beginning becoming the grimmest of fairy tales. But after 15 years and two sons, William, now 20, and Harry, 18, the pair divorced bitterly in 1996. One year later the reticent Diana, who grew gracefully and glamorously into her public role, died in a Paris car crash.

The night before, Charles sent
Diana a note saying "Just look 'em
in the eye and knock 'em dead."

The onetime kindergarten teacher calmed the preceremonial jitters of flower girl Clementine Hambro.

The ceremony was televised to more than 750 million viewers worldwide.

Arriving at St. Paul's (her dress wrinkled from the carriage ride), Di playfully asked of the groom, "Is he here yet?"

This intimate moment became part of the official photo shoot.

Presley later carried his bride
across the threshold, singing
"The Hawaiian Wedding Song."

Elvis Presley & Priscilla Beaulieu

WOMEN AROUND THE WORLD CHECKED into the Heartbreak Hotel upon hearing that 32-year-old Elvis Presley—known simply as the King—had made Priscilla Beaulieu his queen. Elvis met "Cilla" in Germany when she was 14 and installed her at Graceland until she turned 21. The couple flew to Las Vegas for a wedding orchestrated by his manager, Col. Tom Parker. An eight-minute civil ceremony took place in front of 20 family members and friends at the Aladdin Hotel. A few hours later Parker held a press conference in which the newlyweds appeared—Elvis still in his black brocade tuxedo, the bride wearing a $300 organza gown—and invited stunned reporters to the reception that followed. "I was in love," the bride wrote years later in *Elvis and Me,* and hoped that others "would be happy for us." The couple had a daughter, Lisa Marie, but split in 1973.

Bride and groom vowed to "love, honor and comfort" each other.

Streisand directed the strolling violinists not to play any of her music. Said the bride: "I didn't want to hear 'People' at my wedding."

Streisand's son Jason Gould (Dad is Elliott) gave her away.

JULY 1, 1998

Barbra Streisand James Brolin

IT WAS THE SECOND ANNIVERSARY OF their first date, and Barbra Streisand and James Brolin celebrated in a big way. Wearing a crystal-beaded Donna Karan gown, Streisand, 56, married Brolin, 57, in a Jewish ceremony at her Malibu home. The 105 guests included John Travolta and Kelly Preston and *The Way We Were* director Sydney Pollack. A pro at big-budget productions, the bride planned everything from the thousands of flowers to the menu for the reception, held in a 2,800-square-foot tent on her ocean-view lawn. Composer Marvin Hamlisch, an old friend, conducted a 16-piece orchestra. Said Travolta: "It was probably the most beautiful wedding I've been to."

Mrs. James Brolin serenaded her husband with two new love songs.

The cake was an oversize traditional French profiterole.

Some 500 fans waited outside the church for hours for a glimpse of Dion.

Celine Dion
René Angélil

SHE VOWED HER WEDDING WOULD BE THE biggest extravaganza she ever staged, and when Celine Dion, 26, married her longtime manager René Angélil, 52, she delivered. A 17-car motorcade, which brought Montreal to a virtual stand-still, transported the wedding party to the grandiose Notre Dame Basilica for the 3 p.m. service. Once there, Dion almost outshone the church: She wore a 7-pound headpiece adorned with 2,000 Austrian crystals, plus a hand-pearled silk dress (the result of 1,000 hours of work) with a 20-foot train that needed all eight of Dion's sisters to carry down the aisle. (Her five brothers were grooms-men.) Later, the 530 guests were sprinkled with fake snow as they entered the reception hall at a nearby hotel, which had been transformed into a sumptuous Winter Palace. Crowed Dion (who gave birth to a son in 2001): "It was magic."

It took more than 800 workers three months to plan and pull off the elaborate event.

"It was the ceremony of my dreams," said Dion of the communion mass.

Guests partied in a glass-fronted structure on the grounds of Ashford Castle.

Pierce Brosnan & Keely Shaye Smith

AGENT 007 SHOWED NO SIGN OF LOSING his cool when his bride was 20 minutes late. "She's coming," he assured the 120 guests in Ballintubber Abbey, a 13th-century church in County Mayo, Ireland. When TV-reporter-turned-environmental-activist Keely Shaye Smith, 37, finally appeared in a breathtaking Richard Tyler lace gown and coat, Pierce Brosnan, 49, "almost crumpled a little," said his mother, May Carmichael. With sons Dylan, 4, and Paris, 6 months, and Brosnan's three other children, Sean, 17, Christopher, 28, and Charlotte, 29, looking on, the couple were wed in a traditional Catholic mass. Next came the luxe reception at the 84-room Ashford Castle. Before heading off on their honeymoon, the groom said, "Life has been good to us, and long may it last."

Son Dylan lodged a last-minute protest against carrying the rings.

"To celebrate our love on Irish soil, it's the romance of our lives," said Brosnan.

The pair took fitting transport to the medieval church.

Designer Gianni Versace dressed the entire bridal party.

Trudie Styler & Sting

AFTER 10 YEARS AND THREE CHILDREN together, Sting, 40, and Trudie Styler, 38, had horsed around enough. And so, under overcast skies, the former Police man led a dappled white steed bearing his bride to an 11th-century church in Wiltshire, England. Waiting at the altar was a bridal party that included their son Jake, then 7, and daughters Mickey, 8, and Coco, 2, along with Joseph, 15, and Katie, 10, Sting's children from a previous marriage. (All had nagged the pair to make it legal, which they'd technically done two days prior at a London registry.) For the ceremony, Styler wore a $40,000 embroidered white satin Versace dress that took four seamstresses 45 days to create. (It was later auctioned off, along with Sting's custom Versace black suit, to benefit the Rainforest Foundation.)

"Just after the service, suddenly the sun came out. It was like the marriage had cleared the sky," recalled actress Charlotte Rampling, one of 250 guests —including rockers Peter Gabriel and Don Henley—who then headed over to the reception at Lake House, the Elizabethan manse on the couple's 54-acre estate. After a feast of sea bass and crème brûlée, the groom reunited with his Police bandmates Andy Summers and Stewart Copeland to perform their 1979 hit "Roxanne." The festivities continued until 4 a.m., when a proper country breakfast sent the revelers off into the dewy English morn. "It was a very romantic, theatrical occasion," Sting said. "It felt sacred and meaningful, and . . . it meant an awful lot to the kids."

At the reception, Sting serenaded
Styler with a romantic classic:
"Someone to Watch over Me."

Some things old: Jackie wore
her grandmother's rose-point veil and
a single strand of family pearls.

John F. Kennedy & Jacqueline Bouvier

FROM THE VERY BEGINNING THERE WAS something magical about the pairing of the boyishly handsome, impossibly charismatic junior senator from Massachusetts and the beautiful Vassar- and Sorbonne-educated socialite. But no one could have predicted the outpouring of enthusiasm for the exquisitely choreographed Newport, Rhode Island, wedding of John F. Kennedy, 36, and Jacqueline Bouvier, 24—"just masses of crowds outside craning and pushing and crowding in and shoving just to see the bride," recalled one bridesmaid.

Though Jackie suffered a disappointment—her beloved father, "Black Jack" Bouvier, was too ill to give her away—she navigated the ceremony with characteristic aplomb. Looking radiant as light streamed through the stained-glass windows of St. Mary's Church (decorated with pink gladioli and white chrysanthemums), she walked down the aisle with her stepfather, Hugh D. Auchincloss. In front of some 700 guests, Archbishop Richard Cushing of Boston officiated at the 40-minute service, which featured hymns sung by tenor Luigi Vena and a special blessing sent from Pope Pius XII. Jackie wore an ivory taffeta gown and a gorgeous diamond bracelet, while John, impeccably clad in a morning coat, sported a scratch on his face from a recent session of his family's favorite pastime—touch football.

Seven years later the new American President, his elegant wife and their young family ushered in an era of unparalleled idealism. Sadly, the Camelot era was to last for just over 1,000 days.

The wedding luncheon featured
fruit salad in scooped-out
pineapple halves—a novel idea.

"It was extremely exciting
for us in the wedding party,"
said a bridesmaid.

The solemn ceremony included the religious songs "Ave Maria," "Veni, Jesu, Amor Mi" and "Panis Angelicus."

MATCHES MADE IN HOLLYWOOD

*Whether or not their marriages lasted, these stars
knew how to make their weddings unforgettable*

Marilyn Monroe & Joe DiMaggio

THE TIME AND PLACE WERE SUPPOSED TO be secret, but when baseball god Joe DiMaggio, 39, and screen goddess Marilyn Monroe, 27, arrived at city hall in his native San Francisco, they were mobbed by paparazzi. Inside the judge's office, the bride, dressed in a demure brown suit, promised to "love, honor, and *cherish*" (not obey) her husband, as a reporter barked out a play-by-play from his perch overlooking the transom. Just three minutes later the couple, who met on a blind date arranged by her press agent, were the most famous newlyweds in the world. "The truth is that we were very much alike," Monroe said of her "slugger." Alas, the union lasted only 274 days. Yet they remained close friends, and for 20 years after Monroe's death DiMaggio sent roses to her grave three times each week.

Clutching three white orchids, the bride giggled for the cameras.

DiMaggio was married in the same tie he wore the night he met Monroe two years earlier.

"The only shadow cast that day was from the trees," said Bacall.

MAY 21, 1945

Lauren Bacall & Humphrey Bogart

"YOU KNOW HOW TO WHISTLE, DON'T YOU, STEVE? YOU JUST PUT YOUR LIPS TOGETHER AND BLOW." WHEN the willowy young actress Lauren Bacall uttered those seductive words to the grizzled Humphrey Bogart in Howard Hawks's 1944 film *To Have and Have Not,* she foreshadowed a passion that would go far beyond the silver screen. Although they seemed an unlikely match, it took all of three weeks during the film's shooting for Bacall, 19, and the married Bogart, 44, to claim each other's heart. For the next year, the two held clandestine trysts whenever they could. "His first words were always 'Hello, Baby.' My heart would literally pound," she wrote in her 1978 autobiography *Lauren Bacall: By Myself.* Shortly after his divorce from actress Mayo Methot, the two were wed in a simple ceremony at a friend's farmhouse in Lucas, Ohio, surrounded by family members, a few friends, farmhands and the resident boxer dog. Bacall shook visibly; Bogie cried. "It seemed that everything that had ever happened to me had led to this day with him," the actress recalled. The couple made three more movies together and had two children, Stephen (named after Bogart's character in *To Have*), now 53, and daughter Leslie, 50. A tender Bacall nursed Bogart through a fatal bout of cancer. On January 14, 1957, he left her a widow.

Kelly Preston & *John Travolta*

EIGHT MONTHS AFTER JOHN TRAVOLTA PROPOSED TO KELLY PRESTON AT THE STROKE OF MIDNIGHT ON NEW Year's Eve, 1990, the two wed—again, at midnight—at the Hôtel de Crillon in Paris. The couple, who had dated for several months before he presented her with a six-carat yellow-and-white diamond engagement ring, imposed a strict gag order on wedding specifics, but they soon scuttled plans for a "huge" New York celebration when things began threatening to spiral out of control. ("You could have bought a house with the cost of this wedding," she said later. "We had assistants who had assistants.") Instead, Travolta, 37, and Preston, 28, decided to elope, seven months before the birth of their first child, son Jett, in April. "Marriage is complicated, and you can do without it," said Travolta, who had once confessed that monogamy was not his style. "But a baby has to have a real mother and a real father." The Paris ceremony, attended by just four of the couple's closest friends, was so secret that even the Crillon staff didn't know about it until 4 p.m., when a three-tiered wedding cake was ordered. The ceremony was presided over by a French minister of Scientology (Travolta and Preston are both practitioners). "We're not planning a honeymoon," Travolta said after the ceremony. "We go on a honeymoon every other week." A week later, the couple made their marriage legal in the U.S., with a ceremony in the county courthouse in Daytona Beach, where Travolta lived. In 2000 they had a second child, Ella Bleu.

"How do I feel?" Travolta said before the ceremony. "I'm literally high!"

Messing chose an antique diamond-and-platinum wedding band.

Debra Messing & Daniel Zelman

DEBRA MESSING IS ALLERGIC TO MOST flowers, and when the star of *Will & Grace* wed screenwriter-actor Daniel Zelman, 33, she didn't want her "I do" spoiled by "Ah-choo!" So the couple—together for eight years—didn't order tons of buds or take the rose-petal-strewn route to the altar for their ceremony on the grounds of a private home overlooking the ocean near Santa Barbara, Calif. Instead, the bride, 32, carried calla lilies, which are easy on the nose, to go with her elegantly simple gown by Vera Wang. The groom opted for a Hugo Boss suit.

At the reception, *W&G* costars Eric McCormack and Sean Hayes, along with 150 others, basked in the glow of centerpieces made of glass cylinders filled with candles and watched Messing team with Hayes for a rousing rendition of the Britney Spears hit "Oops! . . . I Did It Again." The wedding "was very, very small, and you felt you were there because you were very loved," said guest Camryn Manheim, a longtime pal of the couple's and a fellow alum of New York University's graduate school of acting. "Debra is obviously her own person, but the combination of her and Daniel is just magical." The beaming bride, who was given a 1900 French-cut sapphire ring as a wedding present by her husband, praised him as "the best human being I know. He makes me a better person every day. I'm never happier than when I'm with him." Later she said, "I can't fathom going through the changes you go through in this business without him."

Following the ceremony, the couple honeymooned for a month at a restored farmhouse in Italy.

Audrey Hepburn & Mel Ferrer

IN KEEPING WITH HER TRADEMARK FASHION SENSE, SIMPLE AND ELEGANT WAS THE BYWORD FOR AUDREY Hepburn, who had been introduced to actor Mel Ferrer by her *Roman Holiday* costar Gregory Peck at a party following the movie's London premiere. The wedding took place just a year later, in a 13th-century Protestant chapel in the lush town of Burgenstock, Switzerland, near where Ferrer was working on a film. Arriving at the church together, Ferrer, 37, wore a navy suit with a white tie and Hepburn, 25, wore an ankle-length white organdy gown by Givenchy. While a heavy rain poured outside, the bride held a small bouquet of lilies of the valley and pink sweetheart roses as she took her vows. Though the union ended in 1968, Hepburn called marriage the "completion to everything you've ever wanted and hoped for."

FEBRUARY 14, 1998

Sharon Stone & Phil Bronstein

SHARON STONE WAS KNOWN AS A LOVE-'EM-AND-LEAVE-'EM SIREN, WHO ONCE DESCRIBED A FORMER LOVER——Dwight Yoakam—as a "dirt sandwich." But that was before the whirlwind nine-month courtship that began when Phil Bronstein stopped by the San Francisco set of her film *Sphere.* With the executive editor of the *San Francisco Examiner,* Stone said she'd "finally met a man who was my peer." During a surprise Valentine's Day wedding at Stone's Beverly Hills estate, a gospel choir sang "Amazing Grace," while Bronstein, following Jewish custom, broke a glass underfoot. Then the groom, 47, and his bride, 39, in a pale pink bias-cut chiffon Vera Wang gown, joined their guests in a candlelit backyard tent, where waiters served caviar and Ray Charles crooned "It Had to Be You." The couple later adopted a son, Roan, 2.

Julia Roberts & *Danny Moder*

THE 60 OR SO FAMILY MEMBERS AND CLOSE PALS THOUGHT THEY WERE GATHERING FOR A FOURTH OF JULY celebration at Julia Roberts's 82-acre ranch in Taos, New Mexico. Around midnight they were driven, ostensibly for a drink, to a distant part of the Oscar winner's property, where an assortment of chairs was arranged outside a restored *morada,* a 19th-century adobe chapel. But when Roberts and her cameraman beau, Danny Moder, stepped under a canopy made from white and pink silk sheaths, it dawned on most guests that a wedding was about to begin. As the realization spread, "there was a cheer, a sort of wave of cheers that echoed against the mountains," said one close friend. With coyotes yipping in the sagebrush, Roberts, 34, in an embroidered pale-pink cotton halter dress by L.A. designer Judith Beylerian, and Moder, 33, in a red ruffled shirt and tan pants, exchanged simple handwritten vows. "It was such a magical, intimate gathering, it was like we were invited into someone's secret," said the friend. The next evening the couple, who met on the set of *The Mexican* in early spring 2000, threw a down-home barbecue. "Every time I looked they were smooching and smiling," reported one attendee.

During the 20-minute outdoor ceremony, the couple "made traditional promises in a nontraditional way," said a guest.

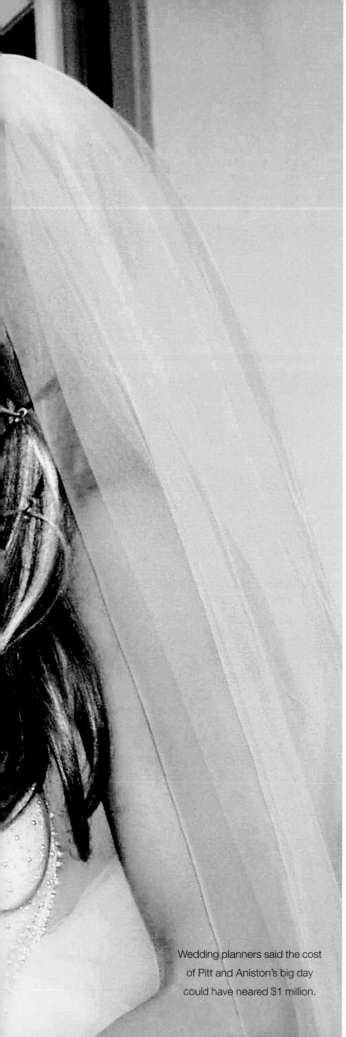

Days of Our Lives actor John Aniston escorted his daughter down the covered bridal aisle.

Wedding planners said the cost of Pitt and Aniston's big day could have neared $1 million.

JULY 29, 2000

Jennifer Aniston & Brad Pitt

IN THE LATE AFTERNOON OF A PERFECT DAY, high on a Malibu bluff, Jennifer Aniston and Brad Pitt burnished their reputation as Hollywood's golden couple. Wearing a sleeveless, glass-beaded silk-and-satin gown by Lawrence Steele, the *Friends* star, 31, strode down the aisle past 200 guests to Pitt, 36, waiting in a four-button Hedi Slimane tux and carrying a pair of diamond-and-white-gold wedding bands he'd helped design. Throughout the service "there was a big smile on Brad's face," reported one guest. The likes of Edward Norton, Cameron Diaz and the *Friends* cast—minus Matt LeBlanc, who was on a film location—were smiling too, as they enjoyed four bands, a 40-member gospel choir, lobster, champagne and a fireworks display amidst 50,000 flowers. To top things off, Melissa Etheridge performed an acoustic rendition of Led Zeppelin's "Whole Lotta Love." "There were big expectations, and this went way beyond that," said a guest.

Lucille Ball & Desi Arnaz

SHE HAD HEARD A LOT ABOUT THE LATIN LOVER FROM NEW YORK CITY, BUT WHEN B-MOVIE ACTRESS LUCILLE BALL first laid eyes on Cuban bandleader Desi Arnaz at the RKO studio commissary, she thought that someone had sold her a bill of goods. "Desi was in greasy makeup and old clothes, and I thought he wasn't so hot," she recalled. The feeling was mutual. Lucy, who had just shot a scene as a dance-hall floozy, looked like "a two-dollar whore beaten by her pimp," Desi said later. But the chemistry began combusting as soon as they sat down together later that day. "There was only one thing better than looking at Desi, and that was talking to him," Lucy said. "I fell in love with Desi wham bang! In five minutes!" They were often separated by publicity trips and band engagements, and Lucy estimated they spent $29,000 on long-distance calls during their stormy courtship. One night, less than six months after they met, Desi, 23, swooped into 28-year-old Lucy's New York City hotel room and announced they were eloping— right after she'd given a fan-magazine interview saying she'd never marry. They drove to Greenwich, Conn., the next morning and, with a brass wedding ring hurriedly bought from Woolworth's, exchanged vows at the Byram River Beagle Club. Lucy's friends gave the marriage six months; Lucy said a week. Instead, their union lasted 20 years and created the iconic television series *I Love Lucy,* the influential TV studio Desilu and two children, Lucie, now 51, and Desi Jr., 49.

The judge insisted on a romantic spot—a club— instead of his office.

Guests feasted on venison, corn bread, collard greens and quail that Fonda shot.

DECEMBER 21, 1992

Jane Fonda & Ted Turner

FOR A MERGER BETWEEN A CORPORATE TITAN AND A SCREEN LEGEND, THE SERVICE WAS SURPRISINGLY SIMPLE. Two-time Oscar winner Jane Fonda, 54, pinned her shoulder-length hair up herself and wore a floor-length, off-white linen-and-lace dress left over from the wardrobe of her 1981 thriller *Rollover*. Outspoken media mogul Turner, 53—who pursued Fonda after reading that she'd split with her second husband, politician Tom Hayden—donned a white suit and shirt, open at the neck. In the front hall of Avalon, Turner's north Florida plantation home, Jane's son Troy Hayden, 18, gave the bride away in front of a small gathering of family and friends. Many thought the match a brilliant one. "They're just so alike," said daughter Laura Turner Seydel, 30. Yet they divorced in 2001.

"I fell for her right away," said Gest, who proposed within six months.

The couple's chocolate-cream-filled cake took 16 people to construct.

"Liza was beaming," said bridesmaid Mya. "I didn't see any nerves."

Jackson ducked out early with Taylor, who was having back pains.

MARCH 16, 2002

Liza Minnelli & David Gest

SHE HAS BEEN PERFORMING SINCE SHE WAS a teen, but never had Liza Minnelli put on a performance like this. For her reported $2.7 million wedding to event producer David Gest, 48, at Manhattan's Marble Collegiate Church, the singer, 56, who had recently shed 90 pounds, donned a showstopping ivory crepe Bob Mackie design. Before a celeb-heavy crowd of 850 (among the 36 in the wedding party: Elizabeth Taylor and Michael Jackson), the couple sealed their union with a kiss of epic length. "I have been to many weddings, and I have never seen a kiss like that before," said Donald Trump.

The newlyweds took a limo to the Regent Wall Street Hotel, where partygoers ranging from Rosie O'Donnell to Kirk Douglas feasted on porcini-crusted beef and a six-foot cake while Gloria Gaynor, Roberta Flack and Tony Bennett sang. Noted Minnelli's hairstylist John Barrett: "Even the stars were craning their necks."

At a press conference the next day, the newlyweds posed for photos in their wedding garb.

MARCH 29, 1939

Clark Gable & Carole Lombard

FOR HOLLYWOOD'S MOST GLAMOROUS COUPLE, IT WAS A DECIDEDLY UNGLAMOROUS AFFAIR. CLARK GABLE, 38, the rakish heartthrob, and Carole Lombard, 30, the feisty bombshell, eloped soon after his divorce from second wife Ria Langham was final. The couple, who worked together on the 1932 film *No Man of Her Own* and kindled their romance four years later, were stalked by the press after Lombard hinted at an impending wedding. So when Gable got a break from filming *Gone with the Wind,* they slipped away at dawn and drove to Kingman, Arizona, where they traded their traveling clothes for suits of gray flannel (her) and blue serge (him) for the ceremony at the First Methodist-Episcopal Church. The doting couple, who called each other Ma and Pa, would not be together long. In January 1942 Lombard was killed in a plane crash. Though he would marry twice more, Gable was buried next to her in L.A.'s Forest Lawn Cemetery.

Benjamin Bratt & Talisa Soto

THE BRIDE WORE FLIP-FLOPS AND AN OFF-the-rack satin-chiffon dress. The groom wore a black Calvin Klein suit. The setting was a grassy hillside overlooking the ocean in Bratt's hometown of San Francisco. And the supporting cast of 20 who gathered to watch the 38-year-old actor exchange self-written vows with Talisa Soto, 35, included the groom's brother as best man, the bride's sister as maid of honor and both the newlyweds' moms.

Clari Soto walked her daughter down the aisle to the strains of traditional Peruvian flute music; Bratt's mother, Eldy, who is deputized to perform civil marriages, officiated at the ceremony *and* arranged Soto's bouquet of white roses. "Family has special meaning for both of them," a friend said of the couple, who were expecting their first child together.

Indeed, Bratt's desire to start a Bratt pack of his own contributed to the demise, 11 months earlier, of his much-publicized four-year romance with Julia Roberts. (Bratt's "a family man who wants to provide," said one friend of the groom's. "He'll be an incredible father.") Soto, a former model who met Bratt on the set of their 2001 film *Piñero,* was divorced from actor Costas Mandylor in 2000. Bratt and Soto "want the same things, and that is hard to find in Hollywood," said the bride's pal Nicky Corello, who joined the newlyweds and their guests for dinner at a nearby restaurant. With Soto, Bratt said, "it's like being in love for the first time."

Both Bratt and Soto "were not obsessed by showbiz," said a pal.

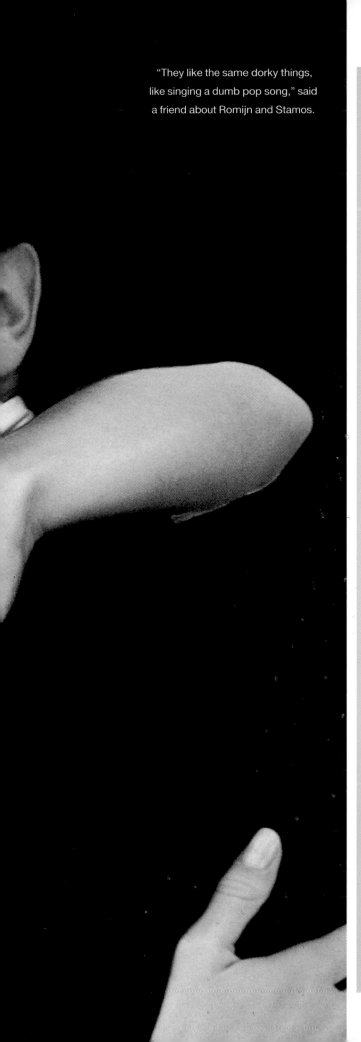

"They like the same dorky things, like singing a dumb pop song," said a friend about Romijn and Stamos.

Rebecca Romijn & John Stamos

WHEN MODEL REBECCA ROMIJN AND *FULL House* alum John Stamos took their vows before 400 guests at the Beverly Hills Hotel, they agreed to love, honor and obey one simple rule: that Romijn, the host of *MTV's House of Style,* steer clear of the kitchen. "I promise I'll never, ever let you cook," said Stamos, 35, dressed in a Richard Tyler tuxedo. The 25-year-old bride, resplendent in a beaded ivory Badgley Mischka gown and a crystal-and-faux-pearl tiara, happily pledged never to try.

This harmonic convergence began four years earlier, when the duo met at a Manhattan fashion show. "There was this big empty white room, and she walked in. It was like a dopey, romantic movie," the groom recalled. Their new life kicked off with a first dance to a rendition of "God Only Knows" by the Beach Boys, with whom Stamos sometimes plays drums. Then Romijn's Dutch relatives traded their tuxes and gowns for farmer costumes and wooden shoes to clog-dance their way through a satirical wedding song roasting the newlyweds. "They sang in Dutch first, then English, then they translated it into Greek for John's family," Romijn said. "The lyrics were like, 'She's a very naughty lady.' Everyone was jumping up and down laughing." Later, guests, including Tyra Banks, David Spade and Rob Schneider, were given parchment scrolls bearing the lyrics to "What a Wonderful World" and asked to sing along. "We had tears in our eyes watching all the people we love swaying to this beautiful song," Romijn said. "It was just joy, joy, joy."

The couple sliced the 400-pound cake, which reportedly cost $25,000.

MARCH 18, 1993

Eddie Murphy & *Nicole Mitchell*

THE NIGHT WAS BITTERLY COLD, BUT EDDIE MURPHY HAD NO TROUBLE WARMING UP THE CROWD IN THE GRAND Ballroom of New York City's Plaza Hotel. The comedian brought 500 guests to laughter (among them, Bruce Willis and Quincy Jones) by doing his famed Stevie Wonder impression in a pair of dark sunglasses. But the room quieted down once his bride entered in a silk-satin gown with a 12-foot train, following her bridesmaids, who wore coral strapless dresses, and four flower girls, led by the couple's 3-year-old daughter Bria. Lobster dinner followed in the Plaza's Palm Court. There, Murphy, 31, and Mitchell, a 25-year-old model who had changed into a sequined sheath, had their first dance to a song called "Cuteness" from Murphy's *Love's Alright* album. "The day I laid eyes on Nicole," said Murphy, whose fifth child with Mitchell was born in January, "I knew she would be my wife."

Sarah Jessica Parker & Matthew Broderick

JUST A FEW DAYS BEFOREHAND, MATTHEW Broderick assured the *New York Post* that he and his girlfriend of five years, Sarah Jessica Parker, were not, as rumor had it, about to marry. "These stories seem to come in waves," he said. "I'd think people would be bored of them by now. They're never true."

Putting off the press allowed the couple, who are expecting their first child this fall, to marry in complete secrecy. In fact, even the 100 friends they invited to the Episcopal ceremony, which was performed at a former synagogue by Broderick's sister Rev. Janet Broderick Kraft, didn't know a wedding was on the evening's agenda. "They just told us to come to New York for a party," said one friend of Parker's from Cincinnati.

And what a party it was. Parker, 32, who was then appearing on Broadway in *Once Upon a Mattress,* and Broderick, 35, who had shared the stage with his bride in *How to Succeed in Business Without Really Trying,* sang along with their guests to musical favorites like "Someone to Watch over Me" and, befitting the occasion, "Love and Marriage." The orchestra, led by the renowned Peter Duchin, played until 2 a.m. With Parker in a black dress and Broderick in a standard suit and tie, the event was classy but decidedly casual. At the end of the evening, each guest left with a piece of cake as well as a note from Parker that read: "Put this under your pillow and dream of your true love."

Being with Broderick, Parker said, was "terrifyingly too good to be true."

Cox wore an antique
diamond necklace given
to her by Arquette.

Courteney Cox & David Arquette

WHEN COURTENEY COX CAME DOWN THE aisle to the strains of Paul McCartney's "Maybe I'm Amazed," the tune summed up the feelings of many of the 250 guests assembled at San Francisco's Grace Cathedral to watch the actress marry actor David Arquette. After all, the notoriously levelheaded *Friends* star, 34, and the wacky AT&T pitchman, 27, would seem to have little more in common than three *Scream* movies and the label—Valentino—inside their wedding garb. But the groom, in morning coat and spats, lived up to his image just once during the 35-minute ceremony. When the ring wouldn't fit on his bride, he licked her finger. (It worked.)

"They looked like two little kids looking at each other," recalled an invitee, who later joined Jennifer Aniston (accompanied by future husband Brad Pitt), the rest of the *Friends* cast and others, including Kevin Spacey, Nicolas Cage and Paul "Pee-wee Herman" Reubens, at a nightclub near the city's famed Fisherman's Wharf. Local actors hired to impersonate stars like Lucille Ball and Desi Arnaz entertained at the tables, where steak, lobster and plenty of Dom Pérignon champagne were served. Two bands kept everyone on the dance floor until 1 a.m.

"David is the wild, crazy one," admitted a reveler, but "he did no over-the-top stuff." With a brand-new bride, Arquette had good reason to be on his best behavior. Reported a guest: "Near the end of the evening I saw him looking over at her, and he just had this silent beam on his face."

"Jeez, what an extraordinarily pretty girl," Newman thought when he met Woodward.

Paul Newman & Joanne Woodward

THEIR COURTSHIP HAD AS MANY TWISTS AND TURNS AS ANY DRAMA THEY WOULD STAR IN. PAUL NEWMAN and Joanne Woodward were two struggling actors in Manhattan when she was cast as an understudy in the Broadway play *Picnic,* in which he had his first major role. The chemistry between them was potent, but Newman was already wed, and his wife, Jacqueline Witte, was pregnant with their second child. The two actors spent the next five years "running away from each other," Woodward said. She became engaged three times, once to author Gore Vidal, and Newman had a third child with his wife. But their love persisted, and within a few months of wrapping their first of 14 films together, *The Long Hot Summer,* the couple went public with their romance. In a civil ceremony at the El Rancho Hotel in Las Vegas, Newman, 33, and Woodward, 27, took the plunge. Blessed with three daughters, they have one of the most enduring marriages in show business.

ROYAL WEDDINGS

With carriages, castles and cheering crowds, fairy tales came true for these charmed couples

Well-wishers lined 10-deep along the half-mile processional route and cheered wildly as the vows were heard over loudspeakers.

Some 1,800 guests watched the couple exchange vows.

Prince Andrew & Sarah Ferguson

DURING ONE WEDDING REHEARSAL AT Westminster Abbey, a thoroughly relaxed Sarah Ferguson kicked off her shoes and slipped behind a piano for an impromptu recital. Yet when the irrepressible redhead marched down the aisle of the abbey, she was anything but casual. Looking perfectly pre-Raphaelite in a Victorian-style ivory silk dress that was embroidered with bees and thistles from her ancestral coat of arms, Fergie, 26, solemnly repeated the traditional 1662 marriage vows in which she twice promised to "obey" her husband. Andrew, 26, a navy lieutenant dashingly attired in his ceremonial garb, smiled gallantly at the longtime pal he fell for at a party the previous year.

Four-year-old page Prince William, whose mischievousness led to worries

Fergie's 17½-foot train was embroidered with the letter *A*.

that he might upstage the bride and groom, proved to be a royal trouper—though at one point he made funny faces and chewed on the cord of his Panama sailor's hat.

When the 45-minute ceremony concluded, the newlyweds rode back to Buckingham Palace in an open 1902 state landau. There, the delighted Queen hosted a lavish midday spread for 100 guests that included Scotch lamb and a 240-pound five-tier frosted fruitcake. The marriage ended in 1996, but the parents of Princesses Beatrice, 14, and Eugenie, 12, remain great friends.

Prince William (with bridesmaid Laura Fellowes) fidgeted in church.

For his wedding attire,
King Hussein opted for a simple
blue suit with white shirt.

Lisa Halaby & *King Hussein*

LISA HALABY WENT TO JORDAN SEEKING ADVENTURE—AND LANDED A THRONE. THE FREE-SPIRITED PRINCETON grad was working for Royal Jordanian Airlines in Amman when she and her Syrian-American father, Najeeb Halaby, onetime president of Pan American World Airways, dined with the recently widowed King Hussein at the Zahran Palace. The two fell head over heels—despite the age discrepancy (on their wedding day, she was 26, he 42) and religious differences (raised Christian, she converted to Islam before the marriage). After a courtship of mere months, Lisa donned a floor-length Christian Dior gown and repeated the words that bid farewell to her life as a commoner: "I have betrothed myself to thee in marriage for the dowry agreed upon"—reportedly $3.3 million. After the wedding, the king renamed his new bride Queen Noor ("light" in Arabic). The queen told a friend that her role "gives a meaning to her life."

Sophie wore a sleek ivory silk dress inlaid with 325,000 beads, by designer Samantha Shaw.

Some 20,000 well-wishers outside greeted the newlyweds.

JUNE 19, 1999

Prince Edward & Sophie Rhys-Jones

BY ROYAL STANDARDS, IT WAS ALMOST A low-key affair when Queen Elizabeth's youngest son, Edward, 35, a television producer, and Princess Diana lookalike Sophie Rhys-Jones, 34, a public relations executive, exchanged vows at St. George's Chapel, Windsor Castle. Most of the 560 guests were friends and relatives, not dignitaries. Said British actor Anthony Andrews: "You felt you were part of a family occasion, rather than a state one." At the reception, Prince William taught guests to line-dance, and the Queen joined her granddaughters Beatrice and Eugenie in boogying to the Village People's "Y.M.C.A." The Earl and Countess of Wessex (their titles were inspired by a character in *Shakespeare in Love*) met in 1993 when Sophie helped Edward plan a charity tennis event. In early 2002 they dropped their business activities to devote themselves full-time to royal affairs.

The Buddhist wedding festivities went on for a week.

MARCH 20, 1963

Hope Cooke & *The Crown Prince of Sikkim*

A COLLEGE PAL CALLED HER "THE COMPLETE ROMANTIC" WHO "MADE EVERYTHING INTO AN ESCAPADE." That said, friends were not totally stunned when New York City blue blood Hope Cooke married Palden Thondup Namgyal, the Prince of Sikkim. As an 18-year-old Sarah Lawrence College student, Cooke first encountered the 36-year-old prince in Darjeeling, India, while she was taking the grand tour of Europe and Asia. Cooke was immediately bewitched. "My husband was a very appealing, very bright man, with a puckish sense of humor," she explained. The prince, for his part, envisioned Cooke as a partner in modernizing his tradition-bound fiefdom, an Indian protectorate the size of Delaware nestled some 5,000 feet high in the Himalayas. After a four-year courtship, Cooke, an Episcopalian who never converted to her husband's faith, was united with the prince by 14 Buddhist lamas in a monastery in the Sikkim capital of Gangtok. Maharajas, maharanis, generals, 12 ambassadors and myriad photographers looked on. The wedding date had been put off a year at the suggestion of astrologers. Unfortunately such precautions were no help. The prince became king in 1965 but in 1973 was deposed and confined to his palace. Cooke didn't stick around. She left her husband—and the Himalayan kingdom—soon after and became a single parent to her two children in Manhattan. Today Sikkim is an Indian state.

"I needed the adventure, needed a plotline," Hope Cooke said of her marriage.

Masako Owada & *Crown Prince Naruhito*

IT WAS DECLARED A NATIONAL HOLIDAY, AND MILLIONS OF ENTRANCED JAPANESE SPENT THE DAY GLUED TO the TV watching the rituals uniting the Westernized Masako Owada, 29, to Japan's 33-year-old Crown Prince Naruhito. The ceremony capped a years-long pursuit by Naruhito, who became smitten with Masako the first time he saw her, at a 1986 palace reception. At first Masako, the Harvard- and Oxford-educated daughter of a prominent diplomat, wasn't interested in giving up her career in the foreign service. Twice she gently declined the prince's proposals. But he tried again in the spring of 1992, reportedly enlisting the help of his mother, Empress Michiko. What persuaded Masako, she said after their Dec. 12 engagement, was Naruhito's promise: "I will protect you for my entire life." Their life together began with a 15-minute Shinto ceremony at the Imperial Palace. Then Masako slipped into a white gown designed by Hanae Mori for the couple's postnuptial parade through Tokyo in a Rolls-Royce convertible. While ultraconservatives had misgivings about a woman who at times walked ahead of her husband, some 200,000 flag-waving Japanese cheered the newlyweds as they drove to their home, the crown prince's Togu Palace. The country is still waiting anxiously for Masako to produce a male heir to the Chrysanthemum Throne. She gave birth to Princess Aiko in December 2001.

The many-layered kimonos were patterned after feudal-era court attire.

The list of gifts given to the new couple went on for 101 pages.

Princess Anne & Mark Phillips

IT TOOK SIX MONTHS TO PLAN THE WEDDING OF QUEEN ELIZABETH'S ONLY DAUGHTER TO HER FELLOW EQUES-trian, the dashing Capt. Mark Phillips, 25, of the Queen's Dragoon Guards. But the outspoken Princess Anne, 23, managed to simplify family tradition. She dispensed with the typical legion of bridal atten-dants, opting instead for just one bridesmaid and one page boy. "I know what it's like having yards of uncontrollable children," she explained. In place of the usual royal designers, the bride relied on the less well known Maureen Baker, who created an ivory silk gown with a molded bodice. And her wedding cake was concocted not by a famous baker but by the Army Catering Corps. Yet the Westminster Abbey service retained sufficient pomp to enthrall 500 million TV viewers around the world—and reportedly gave an enormous boost to color television sales in Great Britain. The marriage unraveled in 1989, after producing two children, Peter, now 24, and Zara, 21.

Some 300 guests went through 600 bottles of champagne.

Rita Hayworth & Prince Aly Khan

FOR JET-SET PLAYBOY ALY KHAN, MEETING screen goddess Rita Hayworth at a Riviera party was a fantasy come true. The love-drunk Khan, millionaire son of Aga Khan III, energetically courted the actress, sending roses to her hotel every day. Less than a year later, amid a press frenzy of epic proportions, the couple said their *ouis* in an eight-minute civil ceremony near his château in the South of France. Hayworth wore a pale blue crepe dress, copies of which (at $18.74 each) flew off shelves of U.S. shops. Rita and Aly drove in a white convertible Cadillac to his estate, where thousands of carnations, spelling out the newlyweds' initials, floated in the swimming pool. Gossip columnist Louella Parsons declared the marriage (which lasted two years) "the most colorful and really fabulous Cinderella story ever to come out of Hollywood."

"I can hardly think. I'm sort of lost in a dreamworld," Hayworth said at the reception.

The bride's silver lamé gown, trimmed with maribou feathers, was by Christian Dior.

Soraya Esfandiari & The Shah of Iran

THE SHAH OF IRAN, WHO DIVORCED HIS first wife, Fawzia, because she did not bear a son, was in the market for a new bride—and his sister did the shopping. While staying in London, Princess Shams came across a photo of teenage beauty Soraya Esfandiari, daughter of an Iranian tribal leader and his German wife. The princess took Soraya under her wing, showing her around London and Paris. Soraya then traveled to Tehran and met Mohammed Reza Pahlavi at a dinner party. The 31-year-old ruler, dressed in military regalia, instantly captured the 18-year-old's heart; without hesitating, Soraya accepted his proposal. On their wedding day the Shah solicitously lightened her load by having a lady-in-waiting shorten the jewel-encrusted train of her gown. Seven years later he divorced the almond-eyed queen because she, too, could not give him an heir.

The Shah's sister Princess Shams walked with Soraya into the ceremony.

MULTIPLE MARRIAGES

Ever the optimists, these serial monogamists said I do, I do, I do, I do, I do . . .

4 **1959-64** For her vows to Eddie Fisher (after he divorced Debbie Reynolds), Taylor converted to Judaism.

5 **1964-74** Nine days after divorcing Fisher, she and Richard Burton became simply "Lizandick."

6 **1975-76** Unable to stay apart, the Burtons re-wed in Botswana, Africa. It lasted just 10 months.

Elizabeth Taylor

AT 18, THE VIOLET-EYED ACTRESS tied the knot for the first of eight times, with hotel heir Nicky Hilton. But she could count the real loves of her life on just two (bejeweled) fingers: producer Mike Todd, who perished in a plane crash, and Welsh actor Richard Burton, whom she married twice. Their incendiary romance, which ignited on the set of *Cleopatra* while Taylor was married to singer Eddie Fisher, prompted the Vatican to brand her a "vamp who destroys families and devours husbands." Undaunted, Liz and Dick resolutely wed in Montreal in 1964. "We are hardly apart, and when we are it's agony," she said. As Mr. and Mrs., the couple jointly earned more than $50 million, and Burton showered her with a carload of gems. In the end, alcohol tore them apart, but "we continued to love each other," she said. Taylor's last union, to truck driver Larry Fortensky, left her disenchanted with wedlock. "Never again!" pledged the still-single Taylor in 1997.

3 **1957-58** The death of Michael Todd (father of her daughter Liza) left her feeling "like a half pair of scissors."

7 **1976-82** Being "Mrs. Senator" was the loneliest time of her life, Taylor later said of marriage to John Warner.

2 **1952-57** "I'm afraid I sort of henpecked him," Taylor said of Michael Wilding, father of her two sons.

8 **1991-96** Taylor wed Larry Fortensky at Michael Jackson's Neverland ranch. Cost: $1.5 million.

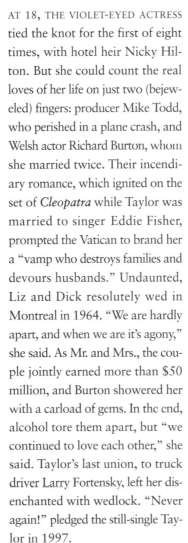

Frank Sinatra

FRANK SINATRA NOT ONLY ROMANCED SOME OF THE world's most glamorous women, he managed to say "I do, baby" to four. Though first wife Nancy made him a father (of daughters Nancy and Tina and son Frank Jr.), it was wife number two, sultry screen goddess Ava Gardner, who turned Ol' Blue Eyes into the consummate torch singer: She broke his heart. After his stormy six-year marriage to the siren dubbed Hurricane Ava ended in 1957, Sinatra exclaimed, "Man, if I could only get her out of my plasma!" The Rat Pack leader tried, with an inexplicable, short-lived marriage to 21-year-old Mia Farrow ("I've got scotch older than Mia," quipped pal Dean Martin of the 30-year age gap) and a last marriage to Barbara, the ex-wife of Zeppo Marx. Seemingly content, he nevertheless carried a torch for Gardner that burned until his 1998 death. "I'm supposed to have a Ph.D. on the subject of women," he once confessed. "But the truth is I've flunked more often than not. I'm very fond of women; I admire them. But, like all men, I don't understand them."

2 **1951-57** Divorced the week before, he wed Ava Gardner and exclaimed, "We finally made it!"

3 **1966-68** Mia Farrow's refusal to cut short work on *Rosemary's Baby* helped end her marriage to Sinatra.

4 **1976-98** Barbara Marx shared Sinatra's Palm Springs home before getting a $360,000 engagement ring.

1937-41 Married to Turkish diplomat Burhan Belge at 15, Gabor said she was "ripe for romance and intrigue."

1942-48 Six years with hotel heir Conrad Hilton produced Gabor's only child, daughter Francesca.

Zsa Zsa Gabor

ZSA ZSA GABOR'S AUTOBIOGRAPHY was aptly titled *One Lifetime Is Not Enough*. Certainly one man proved insufficient for the divorced Hungarian-born girl who arrived in Hollywood in 1941, ready for fame and a second husband. She found the former in movies and the latter in hotel magnate Conrad Hilton before notching up seven more husbands, including actor George Sanders, her divorce attorney and the prince currently sharing her Bel Air home. "Men and marriage," she wrote, "continued to seek me out."

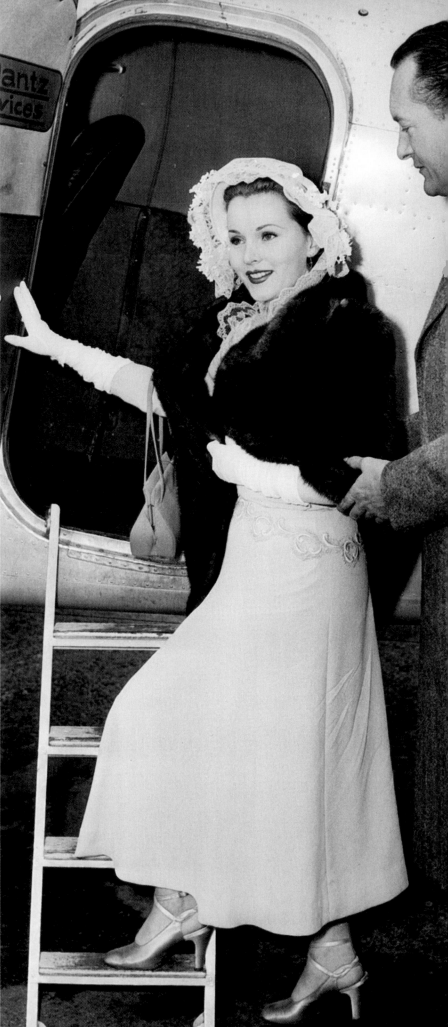

1962-66 As a parting gift, Gabor gave industrialist Herbert Hutner a Rolls-Royce; she got pearls.

1977-82 Lawyer Michael O'Hara handled Gabor's split from Ryan and ended up with more than a client.

3 **1949-54** The vivacious star called difficult British actor George Sanders "the love of my life."

1966-67 A week after her quickie divorce from Hutner, Gabor wed Texas oilman Joshua Cosden.

1982-82 Gabor's yachtboard wedding to Felipe de Alba was declared invalid after one day.

1975-76 Jack Ryan, inventor of Chatty Cathy dolls, wouldn't give up his two mistresses.

1986-present From Frederick von Anhalt, the ageless star got a German title: Duchess of Saxony.

3 **1949-51** Rooney and Martha Vickers exchanged rings with the inscription "Today, tomorrow, always. I love you."

4 **1952-58** A month after she met Rooney, Elaine Mahnken accepted one of his frequent proposals.

2 **1944-49** The actor wed Betty Jane Rase a week after they met, then returned to Army basic training camp.

1 **1942-43** An MGM press agent accompanied Rooney and Ava Gardner on their honeymoon.

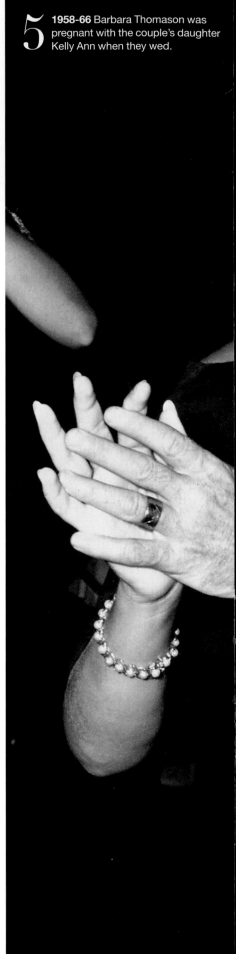

5 **1958-66** Barbara Thomason was pregnant with the couple's daughter Kelly Ann when they wed.

Mickey Rooney

"WEDDINGS?" MICKEY ROONEY once asked. "I've been to a lot of them." From 1942, when Hollywood's 21-year-old boy next door wed 19-year-old sex symbol Ava Gardner, to 1978, when he and his current wife, singer-songwriter Jan Chamberlin, got hitched, Rooney tied the knot—albeit loosely— eight times. "My partners weren't what we call in horse-racing parlance 'routers,'" he said. "They were sprinters. They couldn't go the distance." Gardner filed for divorce 16 months after the wedding. Rooney had two sons with second wife Betty Jane Rase before they split five years later. His next five mergers lasted from 100 days (Margie Lane) to eight years (Barbara Thomason, who was found with her lover in a murder-suicide in Rooney's L.A. home). "The fact is," he once said, "man was not meant to live alone. That's why I persisted and finally found Jan." Not that the father of nine regrets marrying any of his wives: "I loved every one of them."

6 **1966-67** Distraught after Thomason's death, the actor married her best friend Margie Lane just months later.

7 **1969-74** Carolyn Hockett was 23 years younger than her love-bead-wearing husband.

8 **1978-present** When he married Jan Chamberlin, Rooney told himself, "This time it's for keeps." It was.

2 1963-71 The actress wed singer Anthony Newley several months after their first date, which Newley chronicled in a home movie.

3 1972-83 Ronald Kass, a music and film producer, wanted to marry Collins "almost from the moment we'd met," she said.

Joan Collins

IN 1986 *TONIGHT SHOW* GUEST HOST JOAN RIVERS ASKED JOAN COLLINS, "IS IT TRUE THAT THE towels in your house are marked His, Hers and Next?"—to which the serial bride replied, "Darling, I don't bother to have anything embroidered on them. Nobody's ever lasted that long." The British-born actress, who has said "I do" in every decade but one since the '50s, was exaggerating, slightly. While her first marriage, to Anglo-Irish film star Maxwell Reed, was doomed when he reportedly tried to sell her to an Arab sheikh shortly after their wedding, not all were hit-and-run affairs. She and husband number two, Anthony Newley, were together eight years and had two children, Sacha and Tara. Her 11-year marriage to Ronald Kass produced daughter Katy. Alas, Collins lasted just a year with Peter Holm, the Swedish pop star who sued her for $2.6 million after she had the marriage annulled (he won $180,000). Still, in February 2002 the 68-year-old Collins, resplendent in a lilac silk gown created by Nolan Miller (her *Dynasty* designer), wed theater manager Percy Gibson, 36, in a lavish affair at London's Claridge's hotel. And why not? "Quite frankly," she has said, "I really like being married."

4 1985-86 According to Collins, Peter Holm "wept buckets" during their brief ceremony at the Little White Chapel in Las Vegas.

5 2002-present The actress bet the fifth time's the charm, turning down Percy Gibson's suggestion of a prenup.

Caroline Kennedy & Edwin Schlossberg

THE PUBLICITY-SHY MOTHER OF THE BRIDE swore guests to secrecy, but somehow more than 1,000 spectators turned up at Our Lady of Victory Church in Centerville, Massachusetts, to see law student Caroline Kennedy, 28, marry artist and businessman Edwin Schlossberg, 41. The bride paid tribute to her Irish heritage in a Carolina Herrera gown of silk organza appliquéd with shamrocks; the groom wore a blue linen suit by designer Willi Smith. More than 400 guests attended the reception at the Kennedy compound in Hyannisport, where Sen. Edward Kennedy, who gave away the bride, toasted his niece and her mother, Jackie. "I know my brother Jack is here tonight," he said. "I'm sure he'd say, 'Jackie, I love you, and Caroline, I'm very proud of you.'" Continuing the Camelot legacy, the couple produced three children.

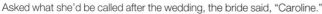

Asked what she'd be called after the wedding, the bride said, "Caroline."

A waving Caroline, with Uncle Ted Kennedy, revealed a temporary shamrock tattoo on her right forearm.

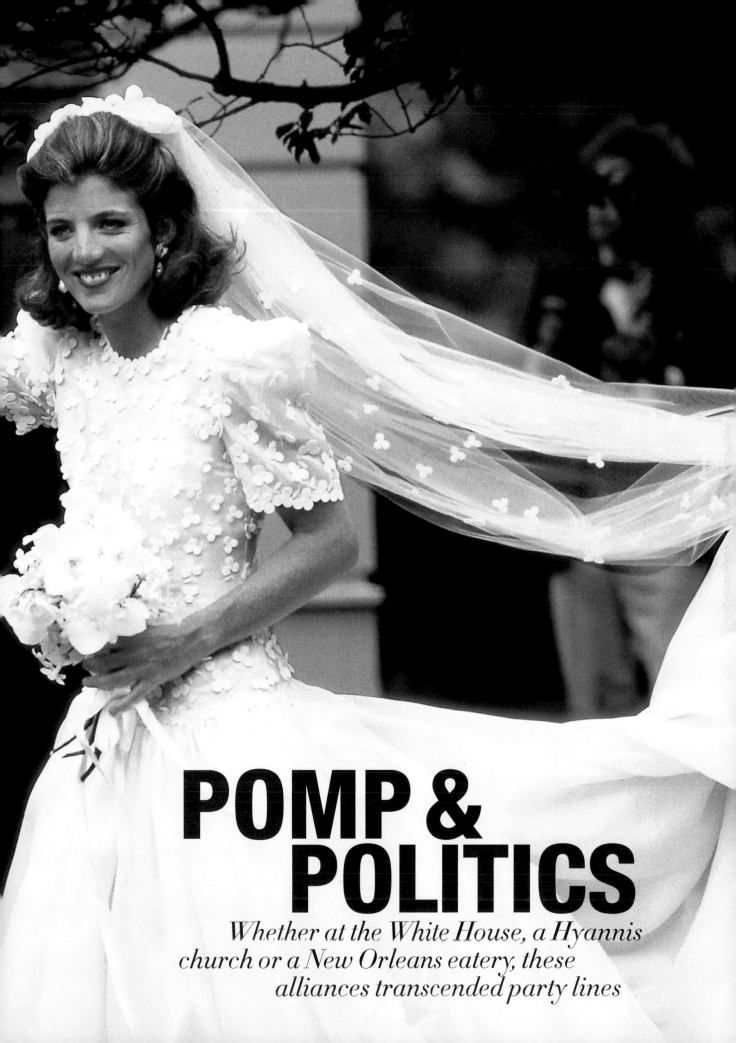

POMP & POLITICS

Whether at the White House, a Hyannis church or a New Orleans eatery, these alliances transcended party lines

Kennedy began bringing
Bessette to Cumberland Island
during their dating days.

John F. Kennedy Jr. & Carolyn Bessette

THOUGH IT WAS AS CLOSE AS OUR NATION comes to a royal wedding, most Americans didn't find out that their prince had wed his princess until after John F. Kennedy Jr. and Carolyn Bessette emerged from a humble wooden chapel on remote Cumberland Island, population fewer than 50, off the Georgia coast. The picture of them doing so quickly became iconic: Kennedy, 35, wearing a cornflower boutonniere in his blue Gordon Henderson suit, kissing the gloved hand of the beaming bride, 30, in a bias-cut sheath by Narciso Rodriguez. Inside, by candlelight, the pair had wed before some 40 friends and family members. Before everyone headed to the island's one hotel, the Greyfield Inn, a gospel singer performed "Amazing Grace." It would be sung again three years later, after the pair perished when a plane piloted by John crashed into the Atlantic en route to another Kennedy wedding.

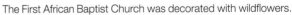
The First African Baptist Church was decorated with wildflowers.

With the President and First Lady standing by, the bride and groom tackled the 13-tier, 300-lb. cake.

Luci weathered the heat better than her sister Lynda (left), who became faint during the lengthy ceremony.

AUGUST 6, 1966

Luci Baines Johnson & Patrick Nugent

LOOKING BACK, THE YOUNGER DAUGHTER of President Lyndon Johnson would say she married at 19 to escape "the fishbowl that was the White House." But her showy wedding to National Guardsman Patrick Nugent, 23, put her squarely in the public eye. Some 55 million tuned in to watch as, under a sweltering noontime Washington sun, 12 bridesmaids arrived at the National Shrine of the Immaculate Conception swathed in yards of pink tulle, followed by Luci in a Priscilla gown with a 9-foot train. After a solemn hour-plus Catholic mass, the couple, who met through a friend, hosted a buoyant White House reception for 700. The bride's sister Lynda, escorted by actor George Hamilton, snagged the bouquet, and the President predicted Luci would "have a houseful of kids." She had four, but the Nugents divorced in 1979.

Lynda Bird Johnson & Charles Robb

SPORTING RED BOOTIES AND A MATCHING jacket that said "Congratulations," President Johnson's favorite mutt Yuki was permitted to roam the grounds during the nine-minute Episcopal ceremony in the East Room of the White House. But when he tried to crash the postwedding photo session in the Oval Room, Lady Bird was horrified. "Absolutely, that dog cannot come in here," she insisted. Photos taken, some 500 guests (including Lynda's former beau actor George Hamilton) enjoyed California champagne, lobster, quiche, and country ham and biscuits with the 23-year-old bride and her Marine captain groom, 28. The couple met playing bridge while Robb was detailed to the White House as a military-social aide. He later served as Virginia's governor before heading to the Senate for two terms. The Robbs are the parents of three grown girls.

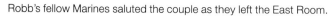
Robb's fellow Marines saluted the couple as they left the East Room.

Before she donned her silk-and-satin Geoffrey Beene gown, Johnson's veil was placed atop her bouffant updo.

Julie Nixon & *David Eisenhower*

THEY MET IN 1957, WHEN THEY WERE JUST 8 YEARS OLD. HIS GRANDFATHER WAS BEING SWORN IN FOR HIS second term as President, and her father as Vice President. They didn't see each other again until 1966, when they were both college students in Massachusetts (she at Smith, he at Amherst), and a year later they got engaged. The 15-minute Dutch Reformed ceremony was held at Manhattan's Marble Collegiate Church, which was filled, befitting the Christmas season, with balsam wreaths and hundreds of poinsettias. The nine bridesmaids (Julie's 22-year-old sister Tricia was the maid of honor) wore pink. Outside, 750 spectators, surrounded by some 200 police officers, waited for a glimpse of the bride and groom, both 20, as well as President-elect Richard Nixon, wife Pat, and VP-elect Spiro Agnew, who was one of only a few politicians invited. The groom's grandparents, alas, were unable to attend. Dwight Eisenhower was recovering from heart problems at Walter Reed Hospital in Washington, D.C., where wife Mamie was being treated for an upper-respiratory infection. NBC set up a closed-circuit broadcast for them so they wouldn't miss the event. Sprigs of mistletoe decorated the buses that transported the 500 guests to the reception at the Plaza Hotel. The groom had the first dance with the bride, to "Edelweiss," but Dad soon cut in. "Julie wasn't nearly as nervous as I was," Nixon said. "If she handles all the great events of her life as she managed her wedding, we won't have to worry a bit." The couple went on to have three children.

It was "a completely joyous day," said the bride, whose lace gown had a pearl-embroidered yoke.

Said Schwarzenegger before the wedding: "We want a private party and ceremony."

Maria Shriver & *Arnold Schwarzenegger*

TO HELP CELEBRATE THIS UNION OF KENNEDY CLAN MEMBER AND HOLLYWOOD ACTION HERO, NOT TO MENTION loyal Democrat and staunch Republican, 450 family members and high-profile friends descended on the Cape Cod town of Hyannis, Mass., and St. Francis Xavier's Roman Catholic Church. "I've lived here since 1941 and I've never seen anything like this," said one resident. Attendees at the 75-minute mass, including Tom Brokaw, Diane Sawyer, Barbara Walters and Andy Warhol (who arrived late wearing an all-black ensemble), heard readings by Shriver's uncle Sen. Edward Kennedy and Oprah Winfrey. Like her formally attired 38-year-old groom, the bride, 30, in a pearl-trimmed white satin dress by Marc Bohan, "was so incredibly calm," said one of the 10 bridesmaids. "She had gone over every single detail." The couple, who live in Los Angeles, have four children, ages 5 to 12.

The rain held off, said matron of honor Julie Nixon Eisenhower, "until Ed had softly kissed his bride on the cheek."

Tricia Nixon & Edward Cox

RAIN HAD BEEN FALLING SINCE THE MORNing, and there was plenty of pacing in the White House in the hours leading up to 25-year-old Tricia Nixon's wedding to Harvard law student Ed Cox. The President had faced many a crisis before, and he solved this one with the help of an Air Force weather report that predicted a 15-minute clearing at 4:30 p.m. Even though the ceremony took place half an hour later than planned, the 16th bride to marry in the White House, wearing silk organdy, took her vows in the fragrant Rose Garden, just as she wanted. Although the 400 guests quickly retreated inside to the East Room reception to stay dry, "a soft rain," President Nixon promised, "caresses the marriage." The couple went on to have one son, Christopher.

Dad and the First Daughter danced to "Thank Heaven for Little Girls."

For their reception, the bride banned cake smashing and the groom insisted on cigars.

NOVEMBER 25, 1993

Mary Matalin & *James Carville*

AFTER THEIR HIGH-PROFILE COURTSHIP AND A RAFT OF "POLITICS MAKES STRANGE BEDFELLOWS" JOKES, Republican adviser Mary Matalin, 40, and Democratic strategist James Carville, 49, made their bi-partisan caucus official. Carville (who was credited with putting Bill Clinton in the White House) and Matalin (who tried everything to keep Clinton out) were married on Thanksgiving night in New Orleans, in honor of Carville's Ragin' Cajun roots. After the 14-minute civil ceremony, a brass band led the bride and groom and their 150 guests in true N'Awlins style from the French Quarter's Omni Royal Orleans hotel four blocks to the raucous reception at Arnaud's restaurant. Matalin wore an ivory satin Vera Wang gown for her second trip down the aisle (Carville's first). "Incomprehensible," Clinton adviser George Stephanopoulos said of the marriage, "but it works." Clearly: The couple have two children.

George W. Bush & Laura Welch

HE WAS MORE NERVOUS AT HIS WEDDING THAN AT HIS INAUGURATION AS THE 46TH GOVERNOR OF TEXAS IN 1994. After all, he said, he had campaigned for the seat for a year, but "I'd started dating my wife and was married four months later." Though the future 43rd President of the United States and Laura Welch grew up just miles apart in Houston, it was at a mutual friend's summer barbecue in 1977 that the Democratic elementary-school teacher and librarian and the Republican oilman finally met. After a whirlwind courtship, they pulled the wedding together in less than a month; Laura's mother, Jenna, handwrote the invitations. The couple, both 31, married in a small, simple ceremony at the First United Methodist Church in Midland, Texas, before 75 guests. "It was in the church I'd been baptized in as a baby," said Laura, "so it was a wonderful way to start a new marriage." Forgoing a traditional gown, she wore a cream crepe de chine skirt and blouse with a spray of gardenias at the waist. The reception, held at the Racquet Club of Midland, was one of several affairs that afternoon, and George Sr., the former CIA director who would become the 41st U.S. President in 1988, "borrowed" a barbershop quartet from the party next door. After a honeymoon in Mexico, the newlyweds hit the campaign trail on George W.'s first bid for office. Though he won the congressional primary, he lost in the general election. But his personal fortune soon improved: The couple's twin daughters, Jenna and Barbara, were born in 1981.

"She's one of the more elegant human beings I've ever met," Bush's brother Marvin said of Laura.

The bride wore an ivory satin Vera Wang gown and carried a bouquet of white Virginia roses.

Karenna Gore & Andrew Schiff

PRESIDENT CLINTON MISSED THE 6 P.M. CERemony—he was flying home from a trip to Europe—but made it to the black-tie reception in time to dance with the bride's 18-year-old sister Sarah. (For the record, it was she who asked, "Wanna dance?") Some 300 other witnesses, though, were on hand to see the 23-year-old daughter of Vice President Al Gore wed Schiff, 31, a physician and son of Republican power banker David Schiff, in Washington's sprawling National Cathedral. One highlight of the otherwise traditional ceremony was Grammy-winning fiddler Mark O'Connor's stirring rendition of the "Appalachia Waltz."

Thrilled with the proceedings, the Veep was heard to exclaim, "God bless America!" as he left the building, where he had been married 27 years earlier. The festivities then moved to a tent that had been set up on the lawn of the nearby Naval Observatory. There the bride and groom were serenaded by Aretha Franklin, who sang "The Way I Love You" for the couple's first dance. Party fare included minted lamb served in tomato cups, one of Karenna's favorite dishes.

The couple, who had been introduced nine months earlier by former Democratic New York congressman Tom Downey, a friend of both their families, bade good night to their guests—an impressive crowd that included Kennedys, Cabinet secretaries past and present, and assorted pols and bigwigs—around 12:30 a.m. Now the parents of two, Gore, who graduated from Columbia Law School in 2000, and Schiff live in New York City.

HIGH SOCIETY

Rockefellers, du Ponts and other denizens of the social set went all out to put on the ritz

"Captured before I went bad, I guess," said Stephanopoulos after giving up bachelorhood.

George Stephanopoulos & Alexandra Wentworth

INTRODUCED BY FRIENDS, "IT WAS LOVE AT first sight for both of them," said one of 200 guests invited to the Greek Orthodox ceremony at Manhattan's Cathedral of the Holy Trinity. The crowd included Peter Jennings, Barbara Walters and James Carville, which wasn't surprising given the groom's political and media connections (adviser to former President Clinton; ABC news analyst). The blue-blooded Wentworth, 36, a humor writer and sometime actress (*Jerry Maguire*), and Stephanopoulos, 40, were married by his father, Robert, the dean of the cathedral. A week before the event, a mutual friend arranged for the bride's family to learn the intricate dances performed by attendants at Greek weddings. Wentworth's ambition, the friend said jokingly, was "to show up George's relatives."

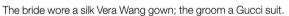
The bride wore a silk Vera Wang gown; the groom a Gucci suit.

Franklin D. Roosevelt Jr. & *Ethel du Pont*

PRESIDENT FRANKLIN D. ROOSEVELT'S SON FDR JR. WAS A HARVARD OARSMAN WHO WAS BEST KNOWN FOR racking up traffic violations and scuffling with news photographers. But he really became fodder for reporters when he started squiring around debutante Ethel du Pont, whose multimillionaire father was actively trying to boot Roosevelt Sr. out of the White House. Underscoring their political differences, a popular cartoon dubbed the couple (who had met at a Groton School dance) Romeo Roosevelt and Juliet du Pont. But in reality the families readily accepted their offspring's romance; Eugene du Pont reportedly obtained the original cartoon as a wedding gift for his daughter. Franklin Jr., 22, complained about the attention, saying, "This is worse than campaigning with Father." Nonetheless, interest in the "wedding of the year" (as TIME called it) ran so high that a few weeks before the ceremony a special press bureau was set up at the Hotel du Pont in Wilmington, Delaware. Some 300 invitees, including the du Pont servants sitting in a choir stall, watched as Ethel, 21, walked down a white satin carpet to the altar of Christ Church in nearby Greenville. They then joined up with 700 additional guests who were waiting eight miles away at the du Ponts' Owls Nest estate. There, as TIME put it, "Jimmy Duffy, favorite saloonkeeper of Philadelphia's younger drinking set, [poured] with his celebrated efficiency." FDR Jr. faded from the limelight, becoming a politician and the father of two children with Ethel.

The senior Roosevelts (left) and du Ponts posed with the new couple after a three-hour-long receiving line.

Mia's satin gown was sewn by her neighbor. She carried white carnations and yellow roses.

AUGUST 22, 1959

Steven Rockefeller & *Anne-Marie Rasmussen*

THE PART OF CINDERELLA WAS PLAYED BY ANNE-MARIE RASMUSSEN, A PRETTY NORWEGIAN WHO HAD ONCE toiled as a maid in New York governor Nelson Rockefeller's 27-room Manhattan apartment. The governor's son Steven, 23, scion to a spectacular fortune, was cast as the Prince Charming who journeyed to Søgne, Norway, to ask for the hand of the 21-year-old maiden. Though some elements were puffed up—Mia, as she was known, really had a middle-class background and came to the U.S. to improve her English—the tale enthralled the public. On the wedding day in Søgne, some 150 journalists and 5,000 well-wishers stood outside while Mia and Steven exchanged vows at the Lunde Kirke, a Lutheran church. When it was over, Rev. Olav Gautestad congratulated the international press for paying tribute to "a girl who has taken pride in being industrious, reliable and faithful." The story ended in divorce after 10 years and three children.

The pair headed off into married life—and a Martha's Vineyard honeymoon—in a 1953 Buick.

Maria Bartiromo & Jonathan Steinberg

DISAPPOINTMENT WAS THE CURRENCY ON the stock exchange when CNBC anchor Maria Bartiromo—"the Money Honey" to her Wall Street fans—wed her own moneyed honey, financial media magnate Jonathan Steinberg, 34. "I don't know what I dreamt of as a kid, but I don't think I could have imagined anything more perfect," said the bride, 31, of the traditional Jewish ceremony and reception for 250 at the Hamptons home of the groom's father, financier Saul Steinberg. Gliding past Barbara Walters and Martha Stewart in lace and tulle by Scaasi, Bartiromo "looked like a cross between Sophia Loren and Audrey Hepburn," said her coanchor Tyler Mathisen. Bartiromo won the groom's heart when she laughed in her sleep, and his toast promised to keep it that way. Recalled Steinberg: "I said I wanted to devote the rest of my life to her happiness."

The blue-and-white theme "was so fresh and elegant," said Bartiromo.

Gates was taken with French for being "independent, smart and funny," a Microsoft insider said.

JANUARY 1, 1994

Bill Gates & Melinda French

AMONG THE PERKS OF BEING A BILLIONAIRE? PUTTING AN ULTRAEXCLUSIVE RESORT ISLAND IN VIRTUAL lockdown, as Microsoft chairman Bill Gates, 38, did for his Hawaiian hitching to Microsoft marketing exec Melinda French, 29. A helicopter patrolled the coast above the tiny island of Lanai to keep it paparazzi-free as an army of private guards cleared the golf course at the luxurious Manele Bay Hotel for the sunset wedding on the 12th tee, situated on a cliff 150 feet above the ocean. "They really wanted a private, human wedding, and they didn't want publicity," said *Washington Post* chairwoman Katharine Graham, who along with Gates's mentor, financier Warren Buffett, Microsoft cofounder Paul Allen and 130 others witnessed the 15-minute ceremony. The formality of the event—the bride wore a $10,000 silk organza gown (by Seattle designer Victoria Glenn), the famously unflashy groom donned a gleaming white dinner jacket, and five bridesmaids were dressed in pink—was in stark contrast to the raucous proceedings the evening before on the beach below. There, during a luau, Gates surprised his bride-to-be with an hourlong performance by Willie Nelson, her favorite singer. As Gates danced wildly to Nelson's "Mammas Don't Let Your Babies Grow Up to Be Cowboys," some 200 Lanaians listened nearby and enjoyed a fireworks finale. Later, from the safety of his publicity department, Gates issued his statement: "We are both extremely happy and looking forward to a long, wonderful life together."

Patricia Hearst & Bernard Shaw

HE WAS HIRED TO PROTECT THE MEDIA heiress turned kidnapping victim while she was appealing her bank robbery conviction (a crime, she said, she was coerced into committing). But by the time Patricia Hearst was released from prison nearly two years later, bodyguard Bernard Shaw was also pledging to honor and cherish her. "We just started out as friends," said the divorced father of two. "In fact, I used to have to go out with her while she was dating other fellows."

Security being of the utmost concern—and money being no object to the wealthy Hearst family—the couple had their 400-guest Episcopal ceremony in the chapel of the U.S. Naval Station on Treasure Island, off the coast of San Francisco. While the bride, 25, wore a white silk organza gown, her bridesmaids, including her three sisters, were in ivory organza dresses patterned with pink apple blossoms. The reception was held at the base's Casa de la Vista, which boasted a stunning view of the city's skyline.

As a 1940s-style swing band played, an endless flow of Taittinger's Brut Réserve champagne was served. Among the abundant platters of food was, as one guest put it, "half an acre of oysters and clams on the half shell." The day was topped off with a strawberry cake decorated with roses and lilies. As for why the April 1 date was chosen, Shaw, 33, explained, "We're just a couple of fools in love." The solid marriage (which produced two daughters) has surprised naysayers. "My parents gave us a Sears vacuum cleaner as a wedding present," said Hearst. "They thought it wouldn't last."

Hearst's Louis XV-style gown came from Saks Fifth Avenue.

REEL WEDDINGS

*When the ceremony
is on celluloid, everyone
can share in the memories*

Bride of Frankenstein

1935

IN THIS FOLLOW-UP TO 1931'S *FRANKENSTEIN*, THE MAD scientist plays matchmaker for his monster (Boris Karloff) by creating the perfect bride—Elsa Lanchester, in an electrifying hairdo inspired by ancient Egyptian queen Nefertiti. But before anyone says "I do," the bride recoils and spurns her intended. In a rage, the heartbroken monster destroys Dr. Frankenstein's laboratory and dies—at least until he is brought back to life in the next sequel.

Funny Face 1957

PHOTOGRAPHER DICK AVERY (FRED ASTAIRE) TRANSFORMS JO STOCKTON (AUDREY HEPBURN) FROM A NEW YORK CITY beatnik into a high-fashion Paris model, wooing, then wedding her. But the true soulmates are Hepburn and French designer Hubert de Givenchy, who created the wedding frock and clothed the sleek actress for the rest of her life.

Gone with the Wind

1939

THE WEDDING IS SMALL, THE MOOD A BIT grim, and, frankly, Scarlett O'Hara (Vivien Leigh) doesn't give a damn. The headstrong southern belle marries sickly Charles Hamilton (Rand Brooks) out of spite after her true love, Ashley Wilkes (Leslie Howard), marries Scarlett's saintly rival, Melanie Hamilton (Olivia de Havilland). Yet costumer Walter Plunkett made sure Scarlett would dazzle even while sulking. Closely following the details in Margaret Mitchell's novel, he re-created the puffed-sleeved satin wedding dress Scarlett's mother hands down to her daughter. A few days after the ceremony, Charles ships off to fight for the Confederacy, soon dying of pneumonia. As for Scarlett—well, tomorrow is always another day.

Woman of the Year

1942

CLEARLY, CAREER-MINDED NEWSPAPER columnist Tess Harding (Katharine Hepburn) never learned how to flatter a man. Just as she's about to consummate her hasty marriage to old-fashioned sportswriter Sam Craig (Spencer Tracy), a deposed Yugoslavian premier shows up in their bedroom—and Tess conducts an interview. Tess and Sam spend the rest of the movie trying to make their merger of opposites succeed. But off-screen the actors had no trouble heating things up, launching a relationship that spanned nine films and nearly 30 years.

The Godfather 1972

ON THE LAM IN SICILY AFTER KILLING A RIVAL MAFIOSO, MICHAEL CORLEONE (AL PACINO) FALLS FOR VILLAGE BEAUTY Apollonia (Italian actress Simonetta Stefanelli). While the marriage is startlingly short-lived—Apollonia gets blown to pieces by a car bomb intended for Michael—the sensual Stefanelli launched a few fantasies. "Some maniacs wanted to marry me," she recalled. And filmmakers flooded her with salacious offers. "I refused so much work," she said.

It Happened One Night 1934

IN THE FIRST FILM TO WIN FIVE MAJOR ACADEMY AWARDS, HEIRESS ELLIE ANDREWS (CLAUDETTE COLBERT) PUTS ON THE right dress to marry Mr. Wrong. Thinking she's been dumped by down-on-his-luck reporter Peter Warne (Clark Gable), she dons a showstopping gown for her wedding to a playboy. Ellie changes her mind at the altar and bolts across the family's estate—yards of veil flowing behind her as she speeds toward a waiting car that unites her with Warne.

Father of the Bride 1950

AS HIGH-STRUNG KAY BANKS, ELIZABETH TAYLOR THREATENS TO CANCEL THE WEDDING THAT TURNS HER HARASSED FATHER (Spencer Tracy) into a mess. But in real life, Taylor relished the chance to rehearse her own upcoming nuptials to hotel heir Nicky Hilton. "Every time we did the shot of me walking up the aisle to the altar, I was living it," she later told hostess Elsa Maxwell. Taylor so adored her silver-screen gown that she wore a similar dress at her ceremony. The flowers, music and attendants' outfits also resembled their celluloid counterparts. For maximum publicity, MGM released the film shortly after Taylor's wedding. Fans lined up for blocks to see art imitate life.

The Sound of Music 1965

TOUR BUSES DROP FANS OFF AT THE MONDSEE CATHEDRAL NEAR SALZBURG, AUSTRIA, SO THEY CAN RELIVE THE MAGIC moment when Maria (Julie Andrews), a novice nun turned governess, weds handsome Captain von Trapp (Christopher Plummer). That scene also belongs on Andrews's list of favorite things. "I've never felt as beautiful as when I wore that wedding gown," she said. "I've never felt prettier before or since. That dress was a miracle."

The Muppets Take Manhattan 1984

HOW WOULD ANY ALL-AMERICAN FROG raise cash to wed the pig of his dreams? By putting on a Frogway show, of course! Overcoming slammed doors, a case of amnesia and a brief detour into Yuppiedom, Kermit the Frog directs himself, longtime love Miss Piggy and the rest of the gang in a crowd-pleasing song-and-dance extravaganza. The till full, Kermit and Miss Piggy—a vision in white loveliness—tie the knot. Asked what other great film couples they would compare themselves to, Miss Piggy answered: "Fred Astaire and Ginger Rogers." Kermit went a different route: "Roy Rogers and Trigger."

Nutty Professor II: The Klumps
2000

GORGEOUS PROFESSOR DENISE GAINES (Janet Jackson) gives hope to horizontally challenged men everywhere when she links up for better or worse with schlubby professor Sherman Klump (Eddie Murphy), the brilliant director of Wellman College's research center. And why shouldn't she fall for a man who looks like a garbage bag waiting for pickup? He's a lot sweeter than his slim alter ego Buddy Love, whom he sometimes morphs into—the effect of an experiment gone awry. The bride gets a bonus when she marries Sherman: His entire family calls to mind the professor—not a surprise, since Murphy plays all the roles.

The Graduate
1967

THE FILM GAVE DISAFFECTED YOUTH A catchword—"plastics"—to express their disdain for the soulless career options suggested by an older generation. Yet few went as far in sticking it to people over 30 as naive college grad Benjamin Braddock (Dustin Hoffman), who sleeps with his parents' embittered friend Mrs. Robinson (Anne Bancroft), then loses his heart to her daughter Elaine (Katharine Ross). Ben reaches the church just after Elaine gets hitched to Mrs. Robinson's choice for son-in-law, a promising medical student. "It's too late!" Mrs. Robinson yells. "Not for me!" Elaine answers back, and escapes with Ben via an ordinary city bus.

High Society

1956

IN THIS MUSICAL REMAKE OF THE 1940 romantic comedy *The Philadelphia Story,* ice princess Tracy Lord (Grace Kelly) thaws out long enough to take a second chance on her first hubby, easygoing composer C.K. Dexter-Haven (Bing Crosby). The veddy proper Newport, R.I., socialite eschews a white bridal gown for ceremony number two—opting instead for a tasteful blush organdy dress with embroidered flowers by costumer Helen Rose (an homage to the original *Philadelphia* design by Adrian). Offscreen, Kelly was preparing to slip into something a little more virginal for her upcoming wedding to Prince Rainier of Monaco. In her new role, she would leave Hollywood behind and work her copious charms on the world stage.

Runaway Bride

1999

THE PHRASE "ALWAYS A BRIDE, NEVER a bridesmaid" sums up serial heartbreaker Maggie Carpenter (Julia Roberts), who has left three grooms at the altar by the time newspaper columnist Ike Graham (Richard Gere) shows up to see if she jilts number four. (She does.) At least Maggie gets the wardrobe right. For her horse-powered gallop out of wedding number three, costume designer Albert Wolsky started out with a long veil. "But I had to cut and cut to make it fly," he said. For the storybook ending—when Maggie weds Ike—Wolsky found a silk-satin dress that made her look "almost like the cover of a romance novel."

Friends

MAY 17, 2001

HOURS BEFORE COMMITMENT-PHOBE Chandler Bing (Matthew Perry) is to marry better-dead-than-unwed Monica Geller (Courteney Cox Arquette), he goes temporarily AWOL. But not even cold feet, a surprise pregnancy and the near no-show of Internet-ordained minister Joey can keep the ceremony from going off without a ratings-busting hitch.

General Hospital
NOVEMBER 16 & 17, 1981

A RECORD 16 MILLION AMERICANS TUNED IN TO SEE LONGTIME LOVERS LUKE AND LAURA (Anthony Geary and Genie Francis) say goodbye to their tumultuous past (the night he raped her; their battle against a world-threatening weather machine) and blissfully greet the future in a sudsy extravaganza staged at a mansion in L.A.'s Hancock Park area. In a campy cameo, *GH* fan Elizabeth Taylor curses the frizzy-haired groom and his beaming bride, setting up 20 more years of L-and-L plot twists—until their divorce in 2001.

Rhoda

OCTOBER 28, 1974

NOTHING EVER CAME EASY FOR RHODA Morgenstern (Valerie Harper). So when the perennially dateless window dresser finally lands her man, Joe Gerard (David Groh), getting to the I dos is no stroll down the aisle. Thanks to flaky former landlady Phyllis (Cloris Leachman), who forgets to pick up the bride, Rhoda has to schlep on the D train in her gown to the ceremony at her parents' Bronx apartment. More than 50 million viewers tuned in, some sending the actors wedding gifts. Even seen-it-all New Yorkers were rooting for their hometown girl. During filming of the episode on the streets and subways of Manhattan, someone yelled out, "You finally caught one!" Harper remembered.

Dynasty

MAY 15, 1985

EVEN FOR THE OVER-THE-TOP UBER-SOAP, the 1985 season finale was an orgy of high camp. The dysfunctional oil-rich Denver clan temporarily shelve their simmering grudges and don their Nolan Miller best to trek to Moldavia for the wedding of Amanda Carrington (Catherine Oxenberg) and Prince Michael (Michael Praed). But just as the couple exchange their vows, machine-gun-toting revolutionaries spray the celebrants with bullets, leaving a bloody heap of Carringtons, Colbys and guest stars on the ballroom floor—and viewers at home laying bets on which characters will return the following season. Shockingly enough, all the principals escape serious, career-ending injury.

The Brady Bunch SEPTEMBER 26, 1969

IN THIS SERIES PILOT, THINGS GO SWIMMINGLY AT THE WEDDING THAT UNITES NOT ONLY CAROL (FLORENCE HENDERSON) and Mike Brady (Robert Reed), but her three blonde daughters and his three brown-haired sons. That is, until the boys' dog chases the girls' cat at the reception. The honeymoon causes even more turmoil. The newlyweds realize they miss their kids so much they have to go back and get them. All in all, a very Brady way of handling things.

Get Smart
NOVEMBER 16, 1968

C.O.N.T.R.O.L. AGENT MAXWELL SMART (Don Adams) has the shakes—and it's not from wedding-day jitters. A map he has swallowed of the Melnick Uranium mines has sent him into twitches—and it won't surface on his skin unless he stands up straight for 48 hours. Problem is, his skeptical betrothed, Agent 99 (Barbara Feldon), won't let him postpone the ceremony. Max manages to vanquish several K.A.O.S. agents in time to say "I do," but he has to spend his first night as a married man hung from a rack. And just when the audience thinks they're finally going to hear 99's real name, someone's snoring drowns it out. As Max liked to say, sorry about that.

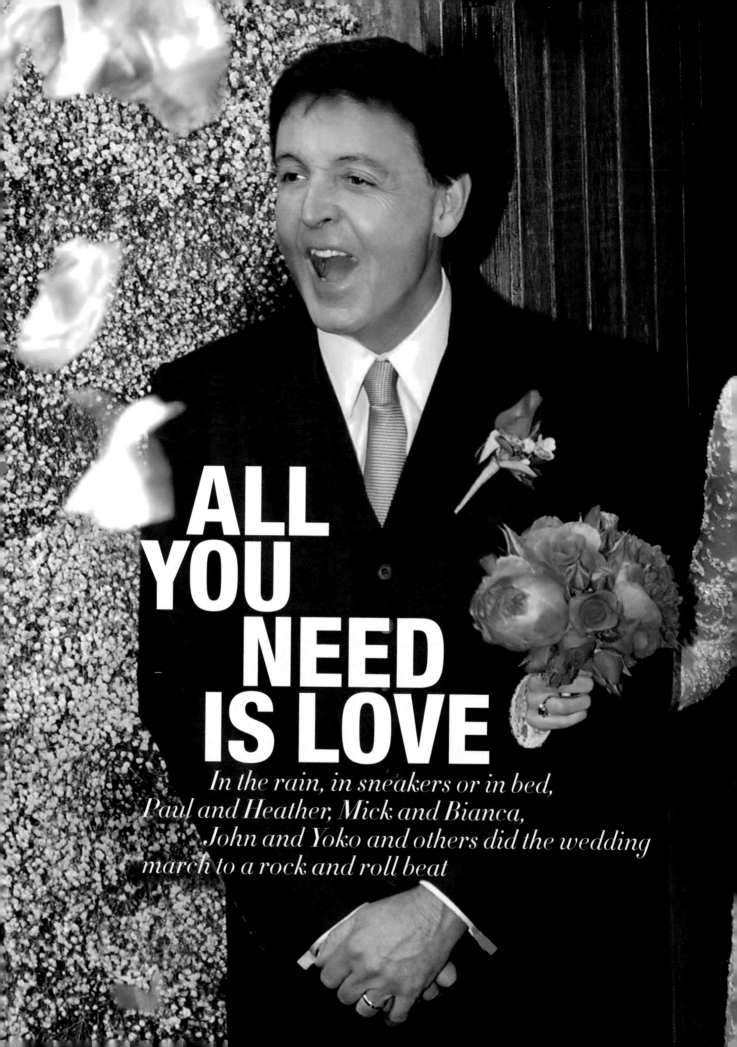

ALL YOU NEED IS LOVE

*In the rain, in sneakers or in bed,
Paul and Heather, Mick and Bianca,
John and Yoko and others did the wedding
march to a rock and roll beat*

Heather sketched the ecru lace wedding
gown herself and had it sewn by
London design team Eavis and Brown.

Paul McCartney
Heather Mills

NO ANIMALS WERE HARMED DURING THE wedding of Sir Paul McCartney and Heather Mills. The famously creature-friendly ex-Beatle offered only vegetarian fare, and threatened to fire any crew members caught eating meat. But just about everything else was available for the couple's 300 guests—including generous servings of romance.

The storybook celebration began at the 17th-century Protestant St. Salvator's church, on the remote Castle Leslie estate in Ireland. As an antique organ played, Mills came down the aisle carrying a bouquet of 11 red-pink McCartney roses, named for the man who waited for her at the altar. While the former model, 34, exchanged vows with the ex-Beatle, 59, "she briefly faltered and wept tears of joy," said a spokesman. After the pair exited the church to the McCartney tune "Wedding March," bells pealed. When the ringing stopped, so did a soft rain. Soon two rainbows appeared—as if they were just one more design element in the $3.2 million extravaganza. It seemed an excellent omen for the couple, whose three-year romance had been buffeted by a British press that questioned whether Mills was a suitable successor to McCartney's late wife, Linda.

No doubts were in evidence as the guests—including ex-Beatle Ringo Starr—celebrated with an Indian feast. At 1:20 a.m. the couple motorboated to the middle of a lake, and for seven minutes red and green fireworks lit the sky in a grand finale. About 20 minutes later the newlyweds climbed into a helicopter—and choppered off to their new life.

"He's quiet, she's outgoing," said Braxton's mom, Evelyn, of the pair. "They balance each other."

APRIL 21, 2001

Toni Braxton   Keri Lewis

SINGER TONI BRAXTON HEADED DOWN THE AISLE AT A LUSH ESTATE NEAR ATLANTA CARRYING A SECRET: SHE was a mom-to-be. The groom, musician Keri Lewis, 30, saw only a radiant bride in Vera Wang duchesse satin and $500,000 of borrowed jewels. But after the ceremony (at which former U.N. ambassador Andrew Young officiated), the admittedly "crazy nervous" Braxton, 34, guided her husband to a corner and delivered the news with a silver baby rattle. "He didn't believe me at first. Then he just said, 'Woooow!'" recalled the six-time Grammy winner. The couple and their 250 guests—including R&B sensation Usher Raymond—repaired to a tent adorned with thousands of crystals for dinner and a cake made to look like a tower of Tiffany robin's-egg-blue boxes. Famed deejay Biz Markie kept the dance floor moving until 2 a.m., when fireworks lit up the sky. "The whole day," the bride declared, "was the best ever."

Mariah Carey Tommy Mottola

FIVE YEARS AFTER SHE HANDED HIM A DEMO TAPE AT A PARTY, POP SONGBIRD MARIAH CAREY GAVE HER hand in marriage to her boss, Sony Music president Tommy Mottola. The gown and the arrangements were inspired by the royal wedding 12 years earlier of Prince Charles to Diana Spencer. Carey's voluminous pale ivory dress by Vera Wang ("a really big ordeal" to get into the limo, the bride admitted) bore a beaded bodice and a $10,000 price tag. (The matching satin shoes cost $1,000.) Attached to the accompanying tiara was a 27-foot tulle train that required six attendants to carry into Manhattan's land-mark St. Thomas Episcopal Church on Fifth Avenue. Some 47 flower girls sprinkled rose petals before Carey, 24, marched down the aisle. Awaiting her at the altar, in white tie and tails, stood Mottola, 43, in front of 16 ushers—including actor Robert De Niro. The guest list of 300 was studded with stars like Barbra Streisand, Billy Joel, Dick Clark, Bruce Springsteen and Ozzy Osbourne. "Tommy has a lot of friends who happen to be famous," explained the bride. Under the watchful eyes of some 200 security personnel, the couple repaired to the reception at the swank Metropolitan Club. There, revelers nibbled on grilled shrimp, pasta and chicken and danced to Motown (the groom's choice) and early disco (for her) provided by a live band and deejay. Though the marriage would last only four years, Carey said, "The whole thing was like a dream."

Despite steady rain, fans lined Fifth Avenue to see Carey and Mottola leave the church.

Yoko Ono
John Lennon

"WE'RE GOING TO STAGE MANY HAPPEN-ings, and this marriage was one of them," said Yoko Ono, hinting at bigger plans. After jetting in from Paris, the Japanese performance artist and the famed Bea-tle spent just 70 minutes in Gibraltar, stating their vows at the British consulate and then promptly leaving. She wore a white minidress with matching hat and kneesocks; he was clad in a white jacket, off-white pants and sneakers. Two days later they checked into the presidential suite of the Amsterdam Hilton for a longer event: a "Bed-In for Peace," which Lennon later immortalized in his song "The Ballad of John and Yoko." For seven days the newlyweds stayed in bed, clad in white pajamas, celebrating their union and sharing antiwar sentiments. "The press would have found us what-ever we'd done for a honeymoon, so we decided to invite the press along and get some publicity for something we believe in," said Lennon, 28, who joined Ono, 36, in giving interviews to the nearly 100 reporters who visited their room. "We are willing to become the world's clowns if it helps spread the word for peace." All the rhetoric didn't preclude some old-fashioned romance, however. "We are two lovebirds," declared the bearded, be-sotted groom. "For two people, marriage still has the edge over just living together." When Ono complained that her $6 wedding band was too big, Lennon drew one on her finger in ink while the real thing was sent out for sizing. "When people get cynical about love," Ono declared, "they should look at us and see that it *is* possible."

HAIR PEACE.

BED PEACE.

Asked if they'd be having public sex, Lennon said, "We're far too shy to do *anything* like that."

To bag Bowie, Iman
chose the tried-and-true:
"I played hard to get."

Iman
David Bowie

A POLICE ESCORT, FLASHING LIGHTS AND screaming sirens led the way to St. James Church in Florence when the world-renowned rock god married the queen of the modeling realm. David Bowie, 45, and Iman, 36, tied the knot in the romantic Italian city six weeks after a civil service in Lausanne, Switzerland. "For beauty, art and the people, Florence is really it," said the statuesque Somali bride, who walked down the aisle in formfitting Hervé Léger on the arm of her father, a former ambassador. (Bowie wore Thierry Mugler's take on traditional tails.) The 50-minute Muslim-Christian ceremony featured music written largely by the groom—soothing instrumentals with touches of saxophone. "We both loathed 'Here Comes the Bride,' which is one of the least likable bits of music that I have ever heard in my life," explained Bowie. While inside was all candles and calm, outside 1,000 clamoring fans nearly broke through the police barrier. Luckily it held long enough for the newlyweds to speed off into the Tuscan hills and the luxurious Villa La Massa hotel, originally a mansion built for a 16th-century aristocrat. There, Yoko Ono, Brian Eno and U2's Bono joined 65 other guests—including Bowie's mother and his best man, his 21-year-old son, Joe—for dinner, dancing and fireworks over the Arno. "This for me is so exciting and so invigorating. I have never been so happy," said Bowie the next day. The bride agreed, exclaiming, "I hope everyone in this world finds their other half, as I did mine."

The newlyweds took the scenic route to a reception in New Orleans's former city hall.

APRIL 16, 1994

Jill Goodacre *Harry Connick Jr.*

APPROPRIATELY FOR A GUY WHO SPECIALIZES IN THE CLASSIC ROMANTIC TUNES OF YORE, CROONER HARRY Connick Jr. celebrated his love and marriage to former Victoria's Secret model Jill Goodacre with a horse-and-carriage ride. Decorated with roses, the chariot carried the pair through Connick's picturesque hometown of New Orleans (where his father is district attorney) after a 45-minute wedding mass at the city's St. Louis Cathedral. After three days of pre-wedding festivities, including a seafood boil and a bachelor's party at the famous Antoine's Restaurant, eight linen-clad bridesmaids stood in the historic church, matched by groomsmen in morning suits. Taking their vows before the assembled were Texas native Goodacre, 30, in a satin Valentino gown she helped design, and the always-dashing Connick, 26, in his own morning suit by Armani. (The pair met in 1990 when he spied her checking out of an L.A. hotel and climbed out of the pool to introduce himself in soaking wet swim trunks.) "Harry's so sentimental, he cried," reported Carol Burnett, one of the 300 guests at the reception at nearby Gallier Hall, where a five-course dinner of sumptuous New Orleans fare was served while classical music wafted through seven rooms. "It was truly a fairy tale, the most spectacular day of my life," said Goodacre. "Awesome!" Connick concurred. A honeymoon followed on a private island in the Caribbean.

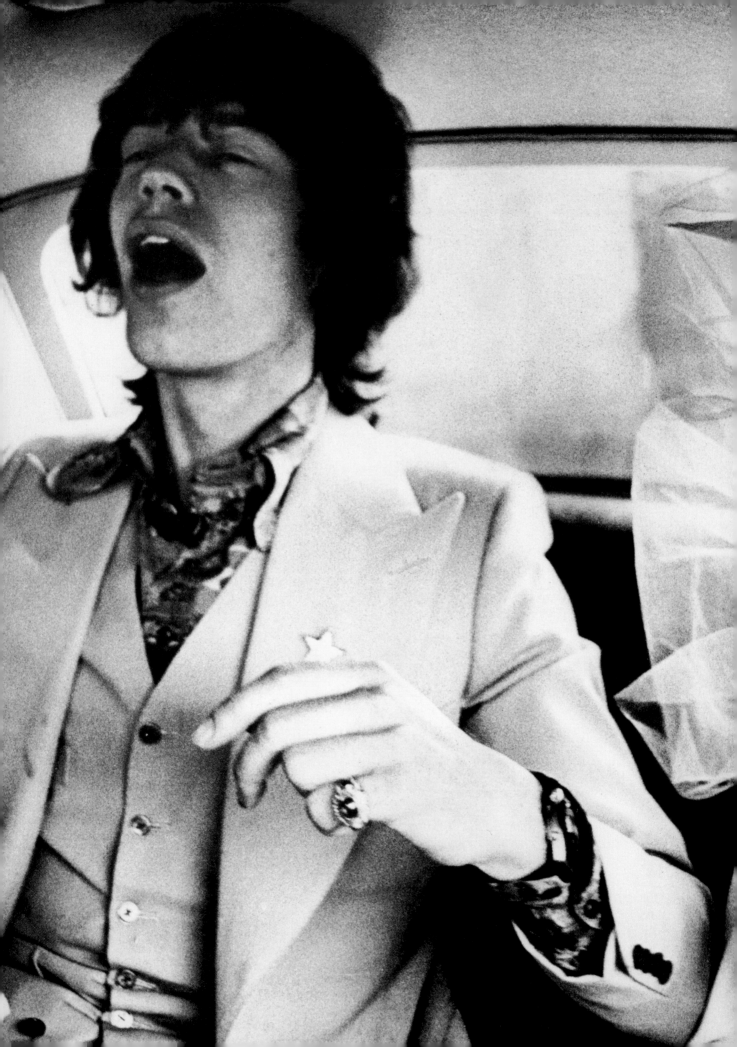

For the ceremony, Bianca had a church organist play the theme from *Love Story*.

Mick Jagger
Bianca Perez

"I DID NOT KNOW WHAT I WAS GETTING married into until the day of the wedding," Nicaraguan-born Perez, a model, admitted. The media frenzy surrounding her marriage to Rolling Stone Mick Jagger in Saint-Tropez—and the prenup he blindsided her with just hours before the ceremony—soon set the former political science student straight. The international press jostled for position to get a look at a who's who of rock, including Eric Clapton, Keith Moon, two Beatles (Paul and Ringo) but only one Stone (Keith Richards). The four-months-pregnant bride, in a white Yves Saint Laurent pantsuit, and the groom, sporting a three-piece suit and sneakers, were 90 minutes late for the civil ceremony, which was followed by a blessing at Saint Anne's chapel. At the reception for 200 nearby, Jagger performed with Stephen Stills. His bride, still seething over the prenup, retreated to their honeymoon suite alone. It was, she would say later, "a bad way to start a marriage."

At the chapel, a Jagger intimate locked the door against the crush.

"I like everything about him," said Locklear, with Sambora at Paris's American Cathedral.

Heather Locklear
Richie Sambora

CONSIDERING THE FACT THAT SHE PLAYED one of TV's most notorious vixens (*Melrose Place*'s scheming Amanda) and he is the hard-rocking guitarist with one of the world's biggest bands (Bon Jovi), Heather Locklear's wedding to Richie Sambora was the very model of propriety. Two days after Locklear, then 33, and Sambora, 35, said their legal I dos in a quiet civil ceremony at Sambora's Rumson, N.J., home, they repeated their vows in a lavish Episcopal service at the American Cathedral in Paris. Locklear, whose nearly eight-year marriage to Mötley Crüe drummer Tommy Lee ended in 1993, turned to Nolan Miller, the costumer during her eight years on *Dynasty,* for her lace-and-satin halter gown with matching bolero jacket. On his first march down the aisle, Sambora (a former beau of Cher's) traded his rock-star jeans for a classic stand-up-collar dress coat. "We love Richie. He and Heather are so much alike," crowed mother-of-the-bride Diane Locklear. The two dozen guests—including Sambora's bandmate Jon Bon Jovi—later repaired to the swank Ritz Hotel nearby. The champagne reception spilled out onto the balcony, where Locklear and maid of honor Lisa Christy, a makeup artist who introduced the couple in 1994, waved to fans on the street below. "This last year has been a lovely growing period," Locklear said. The next week, reports from the Hawaiian honeymoon were glowing. "They seemed like typical honeymooners," said one local limo driver. "Very much in love."

The duo wasted no time getting hitched but postponed the honeymoon (to Van Halen's native Holland) for three years.

APRIL 11, 1981

Valerie Bertinelli   *Edward Van Halen*

SHE PREFERRED THE MUSIC OF ELTON JOHN AND LINDA RONSTADT. BUT AFTER BEING DRAGGED TO A VAN Halen concert in August of 1980 by her younger brother Patrick, Valerie Bertinelli became an instant metal-head when she met lead guitarist Eddie Van Halen backstage before the show. "I looked at him and he looked at me—and that was it," said the *One Day at a Time* star. "My heart melted." Eight months later, with a one-carat emerald-cut diamond engagement ring on her finger, Bertinelli walked down the aisle in front of a crowd of 450 in a traditional ceremony. Both bride and groom wore white, as did the bridesmaids, who each carried one red rose, to match their floral headpieces. A few months into her marriage, which broke up this year, Bertinelli said she had never been happier. "Even when I'm sad now, I've never felt more fulfilled. Everything, good or bad, is euphoric!"

Tiny Tim & Miss Vicki

DECEMBER 17, 1969

SOME 45 MILLION VIEWERS TUNED IN TO THE THEN-HIGHEST-RATED *Tonight Show* to watch the marriage of ukulele-strumming, falsetto-voiced novelty act Tiny Tim (37-year-old Herbert Khaury) to cherubic 17-year-old Miss Vicki (New Jersey-bred Victoria Budinger). Host Johnny Carson enticed his frequent guest by offering to provide the wedding arrangements, including a $2,500 wedding gown. At the peak of his fleeting success (biggest hit: "Tip-Toe Thru' the Tulips with Me"), Tiny Tim sang to his bride and vowed not to touch her for two days. Ultimately the seven-year marriage produced one daughter, Tulip (now 31), and many regrets. "I was more elated by being at the height of glamor than by getting married," Tiny Tim said.

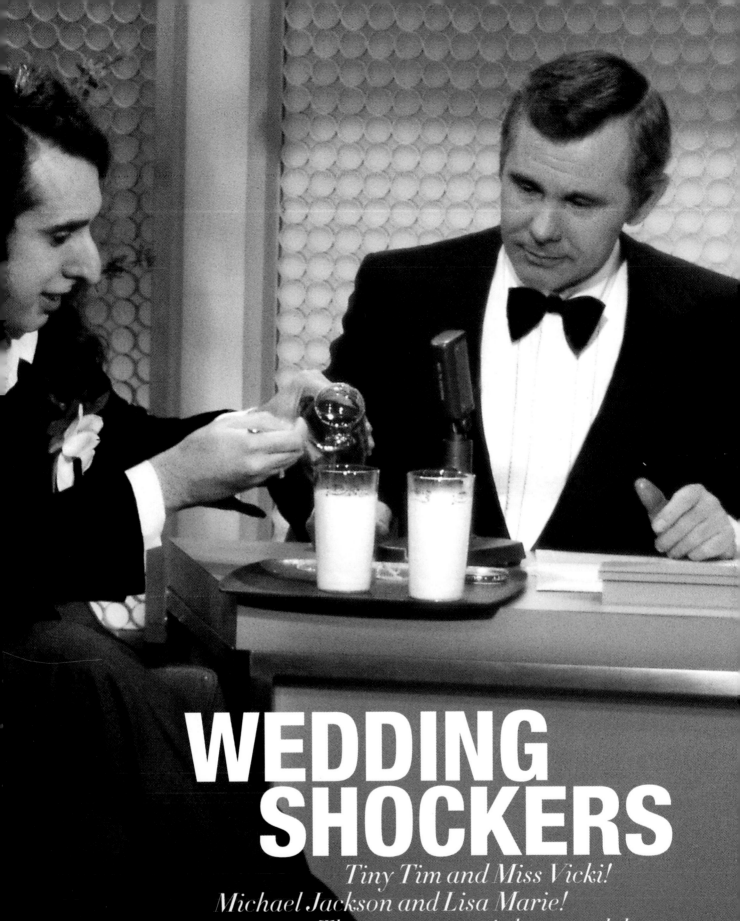

WEDDING SHOCKERS

Tiny Tim and Miss Vicki!
Michael Jackson and Lisa Marie!
These nutty nuptials proved that
truth is stranger than fiction

Julia Roberts & Lyle Lovett
JUNE 27, 1993

SHE'D GONE THROUGH MORE THAN HER share of beaus (including Kiefer Sutherland, whom she'd virtually left at the altar), so the world was astounded when, after a three-week courtship, the Pretty Woman, 25, wed country singer Lyle Lovett, 35. The ceremony took place at the St. James Lutheran Church in Marion, Ind., while Lovett was on tour, and the bride went barefoot. The couple divorced in 1995.

Jerry Lee Lewis & Myra Gale Brown

DECEMBER 12, 1957

HE WAS HAILED AS THE NEXT ELVIS. THEN, while touring in London, rocker Jerry Lee Lewis, fresh from backwater Louisiana, unleashed a great ball of fire by introducing his third wife, Myra Gale Brown, to the British press. The 22-year-old singer had eloped to Mississippi with his 13-year-old second cousin. To make matters worse—as Fleet Street soon uncovered—he had not divorced wife number one when he married wife number two. "Go home, cradle snatcher!" Brits heckled. America was no kinder. "His career was destroyed," Myra recalled. While Lewis managed to make a comeback a decade later, the marriage (which produced two kids) ended after 13 years.

Anna Nicole Smith J. Howard Marshall II

JUNE 27, 1994

"I'M NOT MARRYING HIM FOR THE MONEY," insisted former Playboy Playmate Anna Nicole Smith, 26, shortly before she sauntered down the aisle at the White Dove Wedding Chapel in Houston with wheelchair-bound oil baron J. Howard Marshall II, 89. Still, after her "Paw-Paw" died 14 months later, she sued his estate and, despite countersuits, ended up with $88 million in 2002.

Michael Jackson & Lisa Marie Presley
MAY 26, 1994

ECCENTRIC SUPERSTAR MICHAEL JACKSON, 35, who had never seriously dated a woman, defied expectations when, in a secret ceremony in the Dominican Republic, he took Elvis Presley's daughter Lisa Marie, 26, as his bride. "That whirring sound you hear," quipped David Letterman, "is the sound of a dead rock legend spinning in his grave." In a TV interview, Lisa Marie insisted that the couple, who first met in Las Vegas two decades earlier, indeed had sex. But in two years it was over. "Jacko Gets the Sacko!" blared the *New York Post*.

Woody Allen & Soon-Yi Previn
DECEMBER 23, 1997

THEIR STORY WAS WEIRDER THAN ANYthing Woody Allen had ever written. An older director (Woody) falls in love with the college-age adopted daughter (Soon-Yi) of his longtime love (Mia Farrow), who learns of the relationship when she finds nude photos of the girl in her beau's apartment. While the scandal outraged many, Woody believed he'd found a happy ending. "I'm not saying my selection of Soon-Yi was a brilliant selection," he admitted. But he termed their affair "the best relationship of my life." Six years later Allen, 62, and Soon-Yi, 27, made it legal in a civil ceremony in Venice. They adopted two girls, Bechet, now 3, and Manzie, 2.

Bill Wyman *Mandy Smith* JUNE 5, 1989

IT WAS YOUR TYPICAL BOY-MEETS-GIRL STORY. ONLY THE BOY, AT 47, WAS NO KID. THEN AGAIN, NEITHER WAS PRECO-cious 13-year-old Mandy Smith, whose mother had been helping her get into London nightclubs since she was 11. On one foray, to the British Rock and Pop Awards, the blonde bombshell caught the eye of Rolling Stones bassist Bill Wyman. They began a five-year off-and-on courtship, culminating in a traditional Catholic cere-mony attended by 500 guests at London's Church of St. John's, Hyde Park. But just as the world got used to this match, word of another Wyman-Smith pairing sent eyebrows skyward. Bill's 27-year-old son Stephen (from his first marriage to Diane McCollum) and Mandy's mother, Patsy, 46, had hooked up after getting acquainted at Bill's country estate, Gedding, in Suffolk. The press had a field day pointing out that Bill's mother-in-law, whom he reportedly loathed, could become his daughter-in-law. It didn't happen. Bill and Mandy split in 1990; Stephen and Patsy never tied the knot and bid adieu three years later.

On January 13, 1958, with 500 photogs snapping, Jayne Mansfield and Hungarian bodybuilder Mickey Hargitay headed off for a Miami Beach honeymoon.

Index

Picture Credits